Plan To Win

Plan To Win

Success Guide

For

Young Athletes

Glenn Moore

• CHAMPION SPORTS PRESS •
MILBURN, OKLAHOMA

Additional copies of this book may be ordered through bookstores
or by sending $12.95 plus $3.50 for postage and handling to:
Publishers Distribution Service
6893 Sullivan Road
Grawn, MI 49637
(800) 345 - 0096

Illustrations by Wade Johnson.

Copyright © 1994 by Glenn Moore

All rights reserved. No part of this book may be reproduced, by any means,
without permission in writing from the publisher, except by a reviewer who wishes
to quote brief excerpts in connection with a review in a magazine or newspaper.
For information contact: Champion Sports Press, P.O. Box 183, Milburn, OK 73450.

Publisher's Cataloging-in-Publication Data

Moore, Glenn, 1936-
      Plan to win: success guide for young
athletes / by Glenn Moore.—
Champion Sports Press : Milburn, Oka.
        p.   ill.   cm.
Includes bibliographical references and index.
    ISBN: 0-9637345-0-4
      1. Coaching, (Athletics).   2. Motivation, (Psychology).
3. School Sports—Psychology. I. Title.
GV711.M   1993
  796–dc20   93-72102

Manufactured in the United States of America

10 9 8 7 6 5 4 3 2 1

Book design by Alex Moore / PDS.

THIS BOOK IS DEDICATED TO MY WIFE, FLOY JEAN,
AND OUR CHILDREN, YOLANDA, REGINA, LATRICIA, AND MARC.

Acknowledgments

It is with profound gratitude that I acknowledge the editorial help of Linda Bigbie. Her patience and professionalism in editing this work, and her uncanny ability to organize my thoughts into understandable sentences were an invaluable aid in the writing of this book.

To Dale Callen, who, as a friend, co-worker and supervisor, has given my career his tremendous support.

And, to every player who played for me. Although I was the "teacher", I learned something from each one of them, and will be for ever grateful for the many satisfying years I spent as their coach.

The information in this book is based on some simple psychological principles I used in coaching basketball. Although I am qualified to teach high school psychology, I am not a psychologist and do not want to create the assumption as such. The material in this book is presented to develop confidence in athletics, and nothing else. Emotional problems should be referred to a trained professional.

All names used in this book are fictitious and have no reference to anyone living or dead.

Contents

INTRODUCTION _____ xi

PART ONE

1. THE WINNER'S ADVANTAGE _____ 3
2. THE MENTAL PICTURE _____ 15
3. IT'S NOT WHAT YOU SAY BUT, WHAT YOU FEEL THAT COUNTS _____ 23
4. THE 'YES, BUT...THEORY' _____ 29
5. JUST FORGET IT? _____ 45
6. WILL IT ALWAYS WORK? _____ 51
7. THE TROJAN HORSE _____ 57
8. IT'S HOW YOU TAKE IT THAT COUNTS _____ 67
9. "FLASH CARD" POSITIVES _____ 75
10. HABITS _____ 81
11. DON'T REVERSE THE 'THEORY' _____ 85
12. TOUR WRAP-UP _____ 89
13. GOOD-BYE CHAUCER HIGH _____ 95

PART TWO

GUIDANCE TIPS — INTRODUCTION _____ 107

CONTENTS

14. TOTAL ATHLETIC TRAINING _____ 109
15. HOW TO USE THE 'THEORY' _____ 115
16. SATELLITE VIEW OF THE 'THEORY' _____ 125
17. A FEW SUGGESTIONS _____ 135
18. ONE LAST ENCOURAGEMENT _____ 147

BIBLIOGRAPHY _____ 151
INDEX _____ 153

Introduction

These days, someone is always coming up with a new idea about how to maximize performance in sports. This is a mental training program, but the difference between this one and all of the rest lies in my approach to the objective. In my experience, if the objective is MAXIMUM POTENTIAL, then the real key and backbone to the approach is POSITIVE THINKING.

The coaching philosophy and training process that I have used over the last thirty years is a simple and natural one for both instructors and players. Plus, it has the additional advantage of being incorporated right in with the physical training program: you don't need to schedule extra sessions with your players.

Actually, I look upon my coaching theory as a kind of 'Country-boy' approach. It promotes a positive self-image and develops players' expectations, but without the use of fancy terminology that only confounds the minds of young athletes. In fact, the method can be practiced on a team without the players ever being aware of it. I doubt that in my thirty years, more than a handful of my playersever realized that I was conducting a mental training program along with the physical one.

Over the years, I used this method without ever putting a name to it. For me, it was just a personal way of getting my team to play as closely as possible to their maximum potential. However, to help others understand my theory, I have named it, "The Yes, But... Theory of Mental Training."

The theory is simple and the method painless. It is also extremely effective if used diligently. Coaches and players who adapt the "Yes, But...Theory" to their own particular needs will be astounded at the performance improvement.

I have chosen an imaginary situation to illustrate my ideas and the purpose is two-fold. One, it serves as an explanation of the process; and two, it shows how the theory can be applied directly to sports.

Plan To Win

PART ONE

1.
The Winner's Advantage

**Many have talent, but
few use it effectively.**

I never really cared for field trips.

Even in elementary school when my classmates could hardly wait for the day of a trip, I had a ho-hum attitude.

But, today, as a senior in college, my excitement was building as I and three of my classmates drove down Highway 22 toward Chaucer High School.

To get a close-up look at some of the most successful teams in the entire state was the purpose of our trip. As a baseball player planning to be a coach after graduation, this was exciting stuff.

One requirement of our theory of coaching class at the University was that everyone had to tour the athletic department of one of the local schools.

We chose Chaucer High School.

Chaucer was selected because of its extraordinary winning record. Year after year their athletic teams were contenders for the league championship. Even when a team graduated most of its starters, the younger ones always managed to take up where the older ones left off.

It was a mystery to surrounding schools why the Chaucer Lions were always playing for the championship, even when it seemed they didn't have the athletic ability that some had.

I felt like a detective off to crack the 'Mystery of Chaucer High'.

As a player and coach-in-training, I imagined many doors to success opened if the mystery could be solved.

I had never coached, but I knew there was something more than natural ability involved in Chaucer's athletic program.

Arriving at the school, we were taken into a small conference room in the field house and introduced to Coach Norman, the AD (athletic director) for Chaucer. His job was to oversee all the school's athletic teams.

Norman's size alone was enough to cause four young college men to feel dominated. He was a large man—about six feet, four inches and had a muscular, athletic build.

Fortunately, his personality was not as dominating. He had a pleasant personality and treated us as his equals, quickly putting us at ease.

I had met coaches and athletes who were not so congenial. Some were so egotistical they bordered on arrogance. But, not Coach Norman. I was impressed.

Not the sweet-talking, politician-type, he seemed genuine and down to earth. The uncomfortable feeling we had when we arrived soon vanished.

After introductions, he wanted to know all about us.

Maybe he fooled me, but I think he really did have an interest in us. When we talked, he listened and never interrupted.

We didn't think there was much about us that would be of interest to him, but we gave him the highlights anyway. We told him our hometowns; that Richie and I are both on the baseball squad; Sam plays basketball; and Dean is on the golf team; that we are all seniors interested in coaching after graduation.

I remembered our instructor in the theory of coaching class saying that one key to successful coaching was to earn the respect of the students while making them feel relaxed in your presence. Coach Norman could definitely do this, I thought. Could this be part of the answer to the Chaucer Mystery?

"Coach," Sam said, "we appreciate the opportunity to come here and we're honored by your taking time out of your schedule for us."

"Oh, no. No," the coach said, as he waved his hand back and forth with his palm toward us. "I appreciate your attitudes. The one honored today is Chaucer High School. We feel complimented when anyone feels that what we are doing may make them a better player or coach."

BE A STUDENT OF YOUR SPORT

"We are very proud of what we are doing and feel honored when anyone spends their time to look at it."

The Winner's Advantage

"I'll bet you have a lot of coaches and athletes wanting to visit, don't you?" Richie asked.

"Not really," the coach said. "It's surprising how few coaches and players will ask for advice. Many even reject other people's ideas."

"That doesn't seem very wise," Sam said critically.

"You're right, Sam. It isn't wise," Coach Norman agreed.

He continued, "There are several reasons why they refuse to look at other methods. Some are jealous. Others think their way is best and they just need better players or more time to prove it. Some are resentful. A few feel asking others for advice is admitting weakness and will refuse to do it.

"Some have too large an ego, and others are just satisfied plodding along like they are."

SHARE YOUR KNOWLEDGE

"At Chaucer, we encourage our coaches to be willing to share our ideas with anyone, but also to be ready to listen to other ideas."

"Then what you are saying," I asked, "is that you want your athletes and coaches to be both a teacher and a student of the game?"

"That's a good way of putting it. We encourage sharing because it's our responsibility.

"In basketball, for instance, we don't want them to focus only on Chaucer. We want players to feel they are a member of the game of basketball in general.

"Their intentions should not be to improve and bring pride to the Lions alone, but to basketball everywhere.

"Every sport is an organization within itself, and every member should feel a responsibility to improve it.

"We want all our coaches and athletes to be students of the game. If they will be ready to listen and learn, they will be just like a math or history student—they will do better at test time. In our case, test time is the competition.

"We assume that every coach in the state has an idea that will help us in coaching our young people. That's just an assumption, but it's probably a fact.

"Even you men, although you have never coached, probably have ideas that would help us."

I looked at the others and could see a small smile in the corner of their mouths. That statement made us feel a little bigger, but I doubted if any of us really felt that we had some knowledge that would help Chaucer with their exceptional program.

His next statement really boosted our pride.

"I want to compliment you gentlemen for what you're doing. By coming here today you have done two things. You are showing that you want to improve your knowledge, and you're admitting other programs and coaches can help you.

"I can see why you have developed your talent enough to become college players, and I think you are on the right track to becoming successful coaches."

The coach had really gotten wound up on the subject of sharing and listening. He left no doubt about being serious—actually enthusiastic—about the matter.

"Never be afraid to ask and to listen," he continued. "You see, there is really nothing new in sports. Oh, maybe someone has taken it and added a new twist to it or rearranged it to fit their program, but everything we know today was first used by someone else. All we know, we have learned from others.

"The better student you are of your particular sport, the better your chances are of becoming a top player or coach."

Suddenly, the coach seemed to become aware of how intense he had been.

He stopped abruptly, picked up his coffee cup, and as he walked to a coffeemaker and filled the empty cup said, "I had better get off my soapbox. I'm about to turn your visit into a lecture. I'm sure that isn't what you wanted.

"It's just that humility is one of my favorite topics when it comes to coaching and playing."

He sat back down and asked if any of us had a question.

We all had several things we would like to have known, but Dean, who is always quicker to talk than the rest of us, gained the floor first.

WHY WINNERS WIN AND LOSERS LOSE

"Coach, why does Chaucer win year after year with such consistency,

The Winner's Advantage

and why do other teams and individuals who seem to have more talent continually get beaten by the Lions?"

The coach smiled as if he knew that would be the question. He stared at the wall for a few moments as if he were remembering the past.

Answering slowly, he said, "To tell you why we play well is easy, but to explain it is more difficult.

"The reason any school wins consistently is because they are prepared mentally better than other schools.

"You see, we put a great deal of effort into teaching the fundamentals of a game. We work on passing and shooting in basketball; blocking and tackling in football; and hitting and throwing in baseball. But," he quickly inserted, "this doesn't give us an advantage because every other school does the same thing.

"Winners have an advantage because they have also had their mental game developed. We consider that just as important as perfecting the physical fundamentals of any sport."

Coach Norman had our complete attention when he talked about having an advantage. But what did he mean by MENTAL GAME?

The other three looked at me. I didn't know either, so I took their cue and asked, "What do you mean by developing the mental game?"

Again Coach Norman had that smile suggesting he had already anticipated the question.

MIND AND BODY

Very patiently he said, "I told you it was easy to answer why we have a winning tradition, but it would be hard to explain.

"You understand that we dribble, pass or hit a ball with the body. We also run, jump and lift weights with the body.

"With the mind we control our emotions. We keep our poise, our confidence and maintain our dedication and determination.

"When the mind doesn't have our emotions at the level they should be, we can lose poise and confidence. When we aren't at ease, it's almost impossible to perform the fundamentals with any degree of excellence.

"The mind and body work together to create good play.

"Uh, Coach," Richie muttered, shifting in his chair and wiping his hands on his knees, "there's something I don't understand. Please don't think I'm trying to disagree with you or find fault with what you're saying, but..."

The coach, still with his good-natured and patient tone, spoke softly. "Go on. Tell me what's confusing you. I told you to always be ready to ask. Don't worry about insulting me. My job today is to help you all I can."

Richie relaxed some. "Well, the high school I attended has been one of the best teams around in baseball for years. We were always either in the state tournament or came close, but I don't think there was any kind of mental training there.

"You said that teams which consistently win do so because of mental training. If we had no mental training, how do you account for our success over the years?"

MENTAL TRAINING

"That's a good question, Richie. I wasn't thorough enough in my explanation. Thanks for bringing this up," the coach apologized.

The coach really knew how to keep everyone relaxed. Thinking for a few seconds he said, "What I said was 'schools that win consistently are PREPARED mentally'. To be prepared doesn't necessarily mean there was an organized mental training program at the schools.

"Unfortunately, there's very little formal, mental training on the high school level. That's not to say that teams and individuals aren't trained. They are what I call 'unintentionally trained'.

"By unintentionally trained, I mean someone trained them in a positive way without their realizing it."

"Do you mean a coach?" Sam asked.

Nodding, the coach answered, "Yes, it could be a coach or one or more of several different people. A coach in his normal, coaching style could possibly cause a team to feel and play confidently. If he did, he has given them positive mental training.

"Parents, by the way they raise a child, may cause him to have an extreme amount of belief in himself.

"A community may lead a team to think they can always win by the support they give."

Everyone was quiet. I suppose, like me, they were trying to get all of this arranged where it could be mentally digested.

Coach Norman looked at me like he was asking for my thoughts.

"Then it's possible a coach with a negative way of coaching could unintentionally train a team negatively?"

Nodding, the coach said, "Unfortunately, Marc, that's right. I think it would be safe to say everyone has been trained either positively or negatively.

"If this is true, it's important we offer as much positive training as possible, wouldn't you agree?"

We all agreed, but only by bobbing our heads. None of us were confident enough to speak up.

I doubt any college teacher ever had our attention like Coach Norman. We felt he held a key that would help us become better players, and later, better coaches. Nothing could have been more interesting to us.

His ideas were difficult to understand—maybe just because they were new and different—but he had made it evident he would be willing to go into detail as much as necessary for us to get the meaning.

WHO DISCOVERED THAT THE MIND INFLUENCES PERFORMANCE?

With confidence in his willingness to answer questions, I fired another at him.

"When did Chaucer discover that the mind has such an effect on sports?"

Coach Norman chuckled. "It's not our secret the mind is so influential to performance. Practically everyone knows that the mind has a great deal to do with the outcome of most contests.

"If it didn't, professional scouts would have an easy job. All they'd have to do is sign the athletes who can run the fastest, jump the highest, bench press the most and throw the farthest.

"Superstars could be predicted at a very early age just by administering a simple physical fitness test. But, we all know that's not the way it."

I thought I understood what he meant for I have seen players with a lot of potential, but who never succeeded. They just wouldn't work at their sport, or their interest was directed toward something else.

MIND'S INTERFERENCE

"Those talented players who don't make it aren't willing to pay the price, are they?" I offered.

Coach Norman challenged my remark. "That's not necessarily so, Marc. I admit that many times talented players aren't willing to buckle down enough to develop their potential, but these aren't the ones I'm talking about. I have seen players with a great deal of talent who lived and breathed their sport. They would work as hard as any player, but could never succeed.

"The problem these players have isn't laziness or lack of dedication. It's..." the words trailed off and he let the sentence die there.

He looked at the wall, then at us, searching for the right words.

Speaking slowly and deliberately, he continued, "I don't want to confuse you or give you so much information you'll stop trying to understand our theory.

"Remember two things: One, that it's hard to explain our program, and, two, that the mind and body must work together before excellence can be reached.

"These talented athletes who failed to succeed did so because of interference by the mind. The mind was interfering, rather than working with the body.

"I'll explain this in more detail later, but for now, if you will just accept that the mind can interfere with our ability to perform effectively, I don't think you'll get lost."

I was a bit lost, but was reluctant to ask for more explanation for fear of aggravating the coach.

But, not Dean! He had never been known to be hesitant in asking questions, answering them or letting his thoughts be known.

He raised his hand slightly to get the coach's attention. "Coach, I'm sorry, but I just don't understand what you mean by the mind's interference."

The coach showed no agitation. He actually seemed pleased Dean had asked.

I was relieved he was so patient with us.

"You know more about this than you think, Dean. Have you ever seen a team get rattled?"

Dean nodded.

"Once they became rattled, did they play as well as they did before?"

Dean shook his head back and forth, "No."

The coach went on. "They still had the same physical abilities, but they just couldn't play as well. The mind had interfered with the physical actions.

"You said you are a golfer, right?"

"Yes, I am."

"Have you ever seen a player hit a ball into a water hazard and have his entire game come apart on him?"

Dean smiled. "I've had that happen to me several times."

"When this happened, you still had the physical capabilities you had before the ball went into the water, but for some reason you just couldn't hit the ball as accurately or as consistently as you could before the bad shot, right?"

Dean nodded again.

"It wasn't physical. So it had to be mental. You either lost your concentration, failed to remain confident or maybe became too tense. Whatever it was, it was caused by the mind."

He waited a few seconds for us to grasp the idea, then said, "THE MIND INTERFERED WITH THE PHYSICAL PERFORMANCE."

I had to smile inwardly, appreciating Dean's brashness. Because of it, I now had a better understanding of 'mind's interference'.

The coach looked at us. "Do you all understand now?"

"I think so," Sam said.

A math major, Sam always uses math terminology to describe his interpretations.

"Interference by the mind is like a yardstick that measures how far we are from playing to our full potential.

"A lot of interference causes us to play far below our potential, and the less the interference, the closer we come to playing our best."

"I couldn't have put it better," congratulated the coach.

Sam beamed like he had just got a slam-dunk.

We sat for awhile discussing the mind's influence on performance, commenting on how difficult it is to grasp. Even the coach admitted it is fairly complex.

MENTAL GAME CAN'T BE MEASURED

Coach Norman explained that one reason the mental game is hard to describe or understand is because it can't be measured.

"We can measure how high we can jump, how fast we can run or how far we can throw a ball, but poise and confidence don't have a scale to judge them by.

"In fact, we have such a hard time describing it that we often use words like grit, heart or guts to explain it.

"Coaches are referring to the mental game when they mention mental toughness, confidence, losing concentration and gaining momentum."

THERE IS LIMITED MENTAL TRAINING OFFERED

He continued, "As I said earlier, the majority of the players and coaches know that the mental game is there, but the problem is that far too few do much about it."

I didn't know any of the other coaches in the league, but I was ready to burn them at the stake. I couldn't understand why something so important would not be offered to their teams.

"Why do coaches in other school fail to present this training? That seems unprofessional to me!"

"Whoa, now Marc, hold it," Coach Norman said. "Don't jump on the coaches yet. Lack of determination and dedication isn't the reason coaches fail to prepare their teams mentally. They haven't been educated on what it is and how to present it to their teams.

"But times are changing. Others have taught us. We, and others like us, are passing it on to people like you, and you, in turn, will pass it on.

"Eventually, it will spread throughout the coaching ranks. As it spreads, it will be better understood and coaches will find more effective methods of presenting it, until many high school athletes will benefit from a well-organized program.

"This will be great!

"Everyone knows that the athlete who can control his emotions improves his chances of winning.

"But, winning athletic contests isn't the most important thing here. The most important thing is, that if we can, through athletics, teach emotional control, we are increasing the athlete's chances of success in later life.

"Like winning in sports, the chance for success in life is also increased by emotional control."

He paused, thought for a few moments, then said, "I think we have covered all we need to here. Why don't we begin our tour now?"

PHYSICAL AND MENTAL CAN BE TAUGHT TOGETHER

As we stood and moved toward the door, Richie wanted to know if there were two coaches, one for the mental and one for the physical.

"No," the coach said. "Many coaches shy away from mental training due to a false belief that there must be two separate training sessions, one to teach dribbling and throwing; one to teach confidence and poise.

"Granted, these are two separate components of performance. They are both important and must be dealt with, but they can be taught together.

"I'll explain the basics of the mental game as we make our way through our athletic department.

"As we go along, I'll show you what can be done to combine the mental and physical into one session.

"If you have no more questions, we will go out the back door and cross the campus to the baseball field."

As we left the gym, all four of us walked as close to the coach as possible. We didn't want to miss anything he had to say about the 'Chaucer Mystery'.

SUMMARY

- ✔ Be quick to share your knowledge and ideas of the game.
- ✔ Be a student of the game. Learn by asking and listening.
- ✔ Be humble—avoid criticism, arrogance, and egotism.
- ✔ Physical traits are running, jumping, throwing, etc.
- ✔ Mental traits are confidence, poise, calmness, etc.
- ✔ Winning comes from natural talent supported by emotional control.
- ✔ Everyone knows the mental game affects performance, but few players and coaches know how to adapt it to their own training or how to present it to their teams.
- ✔ How we play is equal to our potential minus the mind's interference.
- ✔ Everyone has been trained mentally—some negatively and some positively.

- ✔ Most athletes have been trained unintentionally.
- ✔ The mental game cannot be measured.
- ✔ The mental and physical can be combined into one single training session.

2.
The Mental Picture

**Success comes from
action, not intentions.**

As Coach Norman led us across the athletic grounds toward the baseball field, we saw a young man hitting golfballs into a net with a seven iron.

As we approached, he shanked a ball that squirted off to the right. Showing disgust, he bent over and slightly tapped the ground three or four times with his club.

"Watch it, Bill, you're smudging your picture," the coach said. The golfer smiled and nodded. "Yes, I was," he admitted. "I'll watch that."

Walking away from us a few steps, he took two or three long, slow deep breaths, standing with his back toward us for about 30 seconds.

"Talking to himself," I thought.

Returning to the net, he resumed his practice. His swing was relaxed and smooth and there was a good solid 'click' as the iron drove ball after ball into the trap.

What the coach had said about smudging his picture seemed to have worked. There was no indication that Bill had just fouled up on an earlier shot.

"What is 'smudging your picture'?" Dean asked.

Coach Norman's lips curled in a little smile. Moving his head slowly to the right and back to the left, he took a deep breath and let it out in one puff.

Richie giggled. "We know. It's hard to explain the mental game."

The coach had done a good job of putting him at ease. Richie had always been one to pick at people he liked, but I didn't expect him to start on the coach this quickly.

The coach seemed to enjoy it. Looking at Richie he said, "Thanks, Richie. I hated to say that again, but it's true." He suggested we move into the shade of a nearby tree. "This may take a while."

MENTAL IMAGE—OUR OPINION OF OURSELVES

"When I told Bill he was smudging his picture, I was referring to the mental picture he has of himself," the coach began.

"Our mental picture is how we see ourselves in our own mind. It's the ENTIRE OPINION WE HAVE OF OURSELVES.

"What is your opinion of yourself, Richie?"

"Why..Uh...I don't know," Richie stammered.

"Oh, come on, now," the coach insisted. "Everyone has an opinion of himself."

Richie had been relaxed, but not now. Nervously he asked, "Do you mean about my baseball, in the classroom, or what?"

Coach Norman laughed, enjoying getting back at Richie.

"Okay, I'll let you off the hook," he said, still smiling. "It would be impossible for you to answer the question in a short period of time. Our opinion of ourselves is very broad. It reaches into every little corner of our lives.

"Anyone teenage or older could fill book after book with the evaluation he has of himself.

"We have opinions about how we are at driving a car. casting a fishing lure, and our favorite and least favorite foods, colors and movies.

"There are millions of opinions we have about ourselves. The list could go on and on."

FEELINGS AFFECT PERFORMANCE

"Coach," I asked, "I understand mental picture and it being our opinion, but are you suggesting this can influence my ability to play baseball?"

"Most definitely, Marc. To understand this, there are two ideas you need to grasp. One, our opinion has a lot to do with how we feel.

"Two, there is a close relationship between how we feel about ourselves and how we perform.

The Mental Picture

"If your feeling of yourself is one of confidence, is free of harmful tension, and you're satisfied, you can expect a successful performance.

"If your feelings are the opposite of this, performance is apt to suffer.

"Imagine yourself trying to get a good hit or make a good infield play while your thoughts are filled with doubts and fears.

"These doubts and fears are your feelings and, to a great extent, are a result of your self-image."

"Oh, I see," I told him. "The picture we paint influences how we feel and the feeling we have influences how we play. That makes sense."

"Good," Coach Norman said.

PAINTING THE PICTURE

"I have a question," Sam said. "How do we begin painting this picture of ourselves?"

"No, Sam," the coach waved his hand back and forth. "Our intention isn't to start painting a picture. We already have one. We want to improve the one we have.

"The painting of this picture began when we were only babies, and is still being painted today.

"The picture will never be completed as long as we are alive. We will be adding to it, taking away from it and changing it for the rest of our lives.

"Every experience we have is a possibility for us to alter our self-image," he explained.

"We teach our athletes that every time something pleasing happens to them, or something that makes them feel good about themselves, their mental picture will probably become brighter.

"When anything happens that causes the players to feel worse about themselves, we call it 'smudging the picture'."

Thoughtfully, Sam said, "Then what you are saying is that when something good happens to us it causes us to have a higher opinion of ourselves. This, in turn, leads to more self-confidence and better performance.

"When something bad happens, our picture is messed up and we lose some of our confidence."

"Not exactly. What you have described, Sam," the coach said, "is an average person, but not a winner.

"A winner controls what happens to his picture.

"Think with me for a few moments. BOTH GOOD AND BAD HAPPENS TO ALL OF US.

"Marc, while playing baseball, you get hits, but also you strike out. You make good fielding plays, but you sometimes make errors.

"Sam, you get rebounds and score, but you also double-dribble occasionally, right?"

Sam and I nodded.

"Dean," he continued, "you make good shots onto the green and may even stop the ball near the cup, but you hit the bunker sometimes, too, correct?"

Dean laughed a little. "Yes, I've been in the sand," he replied.

The coach went on. "Now if it was a set law of nature that the good made our mental picture brighter, and the bad smudged it, we would have no control over our confidence or our fates.

"It would be out of control. We would be at the mercy of whatever happened to us.

"Although most athletes' lives follow this pattern, it doesn't have to be that way.

"We can have more control over situations that affect confidence."

"Coach," I said, "Let me see if I understand what you're saying?"

"Sure go ahead."

"When Bill muffed the shot, although it was a minor thing, we will consider it to be 'something bad'. By showing frustration, he was creating a situation that could cause him to develop some doubt.

"Am I right?"

"Yes, you're right."

"Then I have a question. How could Bill have handled the poor shot without smudging his picture? How could he have controlled what happened to his mental image?"

He thought for a moment and said, "Do you agree that how we feel about situations influences our play?"

"Yes."

"Fine. Now, let's assume by the way Bill reacted to the muffed shot that his thoughts went something like, 'You idiot, how can you mess up on a simple short iron shot into a practice net'.

"His feelings may have been that if he messed up on a shot with ideal conditions, what would he do on a golf course, when the pressure was on and

The Mental Picture

his ball wasn't setting in a perfect position.

"Now, Bill is a good golfer, and I doubt that this one negative reaction will destroy his confidence, but if he allows himself to think this way every time he makes a mistake, it may eventually change his picture of himself drastically.

"And," he continued, "it's possible that allowing frustration to surface only one time could permit a little doubt to creep into his opinion of himself. If this happens, his mental picture will be smudged.

"If Bill allows himself to become dejected over this shot, it will be easier and easier to become discouraged, until it becomes habitual. If this happens, his mental image is in trouble."

Coach Norman shifted his position, then continued.

"The aim of all mental training programs is to keep the mental picture clear and positive.

"I'm not ready yet to get into our program, which we call the 'Yes, But...Theory', because there are some things you need to understand before we begin discussing it. But, what we try to do with it is keep negatives from influencing our play.

"We want to make rejecting them a habit."

We stood in the shade of the tree for several minutes discussing self-image and watching Bill practice his golf shot.

Our discussion, though, consisted mainly of one of us asking a question and barely giving the coach time to answer before we fired another.

SELF-IMAGE IS CONTROLLABLE

Finally, the coach returned to the question I had asked earlier.

"We have discussed some possible thoughts Bill may have allowed to run through his mind. Now, do any of you have a suggestion on how Bill should have felt after the poor shot?"

Dean spoke, "I've been watching him as we've been talking. He's been very consistent in hitting the ball since that one bad shot."

"Good," he told Dean. "Then he should have felt that the one shot was an exception rather than the norm.

"We need to keep everything in the correct perspective. Don't make a mountain out of a mole hill, right?"

Dean agreed.

We all have our mental images of ourself. These images are really our opinion of ourselves. They include how capable we are, how much talent we have, what we can do, what we can't do, etc. But, these images usually don't match what is real. Our opinion is usually either less or greater than what we are.

The Mental Picture

"I know what my coach would have suggested," Sam said.

"What's that?" the coach asked.

"He would say 'use it as a learning experience. Decide why you made the mistake, and then practice it to prevent it from happening again'. He always encouraged us to use mistakes as a stepping-stone rather than a stumbling block."

"That's good advice," the coach said. "It would do two things for you. It would help you improve the fundamental, and it would keep you from thinking poor things about yourself.

"I'm sure there are other thoughts we could suggest that Bill could use, but I think you're getting the idea that we're not at the mercy of what happens. We can control our self-image.

"Just because something bad happens to us doesn't mean our mental picture has to be smudged."

"That's satisfying," Sam remarked.

"What do you mean?" Coach Norman asked him.

"It's nice to know we can be in control of our confidence," he said happily.

WE'RE OUR OWN ARTIST

"Yes, it is. We teach our players they are the artist of their own mental image.

"It's encouraging to know that we can paint a picture of confidence, but you must never forget, we can also paint doubt and fears into our image."

This reminded Coach Norman of a girl at Chaucer who played basketball.

"The girl," he told us, "had an enormous amount of potential, but never materialized into the player she could have been.

"The mental image she had of herself was a picture of a player who lacked the ability to be good. She felt that if she did something good, it was because she had been lucky.

"She could hit a short jump shot and would act as if she had just hit a desperation shot from the center line.

"The coaches tried to paint her picture brightly, but she continued to hold onto that image of a girl who must be lucky to perform well."

He explained that as long as the girl didn't agree with the coaches, it had no influence on her mental picture.

"Your self-image is formed by what is real in your own eyes," he said.

"So, you see, no one can paint your picture brightly unless you agree with what they say.

"This girl did her own painting, but she painted it negatively. No matter how hard the coaches tried, this girl wouldn't let them improve her picture.

"Gentlemen," he warned, "don't take this to mean that we should let others decide what we should paint. This can be very dangerous.

"You may be told you are no good, too short, not strong enough, or that you are crazy to set such high goals.

"These will affect your image only if you believe them. If they are not real in your own eyes, they will have no influence whatsoever.

"There are hundreds of thousands of people addicted to drugs, and jail cells filled with people who let others dictate what was painted in their minds.

"Winners will not allow anyone to mess up their picture.

"Losers often paint any stroke on the mental canvas that others suggest.

"Paint your own picture and paint it brightly."

SUMMARY

- ✔ Our mental picture is composed of every opinion we have about ourselves.
- ✔ To perform well, we need a positive self-image.
- ✔ The mental image influences our feelings, and feelings affect performance.
- ✔ Our mental picture is always changing.
- ✔ Good and bad happens to us all. Success depends on our remaining positive through both.
- ✔ We do have some control over our thoughts during bad times.
- ✔ Since we are creatures of habit, our habits must be positive.
- ✔ We can use mistakes as stepping stones to success.
- ✔ Everyone is the artist of his mental picture.

3.
It's Not What You Say, But What You Feel That Counts

> **Before you run from a problem, make sure there's one there.**

The baseball field was well kept. The grass was clipped around the fences, and the cut-out part of the infield and baselines were neatly trimmed.

Players were working on fundamentals in six or seven groups around the field. There was no goofing off. Everyone seemed contented, and each was attending to his part of the practice.

I wanted to get a ball and glove and join them.

Coach Norman led us to a batting cage where a player was getting ready to take batting practice using the automatic pitching machine.

The player looked like a junior or senior. His build and the way he handled himself caused me to guess he was probably one of the better players.

ONLY WHAT YOU BELIEVE AFFECTS YOU

When he began taking his cuts, we could hear him talking to himself. Before each pitch he would say, "I'm a good hitter."

He was saying he was good, but his swings didn't show it. He would top the ball, driving it into the ground, which in a game, would be an easy ground ball for an infielder or pitcher to handle, or he would get under the ball, popping it up.

His hitting was poor, but before each swing he continued to say, "I'm a good hitter."

Coach Smith, the baseball coach, who had been working with a player on getting a good jump on an attempted stolen base, walked up to the cage.

He stood outside the cage for a few moments, watching and listening.

"Hold it a minute, John," he said.

John held up his hand to the player feeding balls into the machine.

He turned and asked, "What is it, Coach?"

"What are you talking about?" the coach questioned him.

I think John was glad the coach had asked. There seemed to be a lot of pride in his voice.

"I'm using positive thinking to get my hitting back in the groove," he said. "My hitting hasn't been very good lately. So, I'm using positive self-talk to straighten it out."

Coach Smith looked at John a few seconds, then walked to the front of the cage to the entrance gate. I guessed he wanted some extra time to gather his thoughts.

"John, I appreciate your dedication. I'm very proud of your effort in trying to correct your hitting situation, but I'm not sure you're approaching it the right way."

John looked puzzled. "What do you mean? You're always telling us to be positive."

"That's right. But I'm not sure you're being positive in this instance by saying, 'I'm a good hitter'."

"What do you mean?" John asked again.

"It's true that making positive statements to yourself will brighten a smudged picture," Coach Smith said with an understanding tone of voice.

"But, there is one important factor you must always remember. For a statement to be positive it must be something you already believe to be the truth.

"You can't fib to yourself and be positive at the same time."

He put his arm on John's shoulder and asked, "Are you a good hitter?"

"Well, I have been in the past. My batting average is over .350," John said confidently.

"But, your statement, 'I'm a good hitter', is saying that you ARE a good hitter RIGHT NOW. Are you?"

ATTEMPTS TO BE POSITIVE
CAN END UP BEING NEGATIVE

John looked at the ground and moved some sand around with his cleats. "Well...uh...not really."

"There's no reason to hang your head, John," the coach said softly. "I'm very proud of you for trying to keep your mental game in good shape. The more you work at mental training, the more you'll learn about it, and the more you learn, the more effective you'll be at preparing yourself mentally."

Coach Smith, like Coach Norman, seemed to really be concerned about what was going on inside the minds of his players.

The coach continued, "You're saying that you are a good hitter, but you feel you're not.

"You don't believe what you're saying to yourself, so it isn't a positive statement.

"Deep down, you may be telling yourself, 'I'm not a good hitter, but I'm trying to convince myself I am'. Would you agree with that?"

"Probably so," John admitted. "Because I don't feel like a good hitter right now."

The coach, still in a mild tone, said, "It's possible that every swing you took was placing emphasis on the belief that you haven't been hitting the ball well lately.

"You were saying you're a good hitter, but feeling like you aren't. Since what you feel is the thing that affects your mental game, you may have been driving yourself deeper and deeper into a batting slump.

"Your attempt to be positive may have really been negative."

"I never thought of it that way," John said, surprised.

"Remember, John," Coach Smith said, "any time you want to brighten your mental picture with positive words, YOU MUST USE SOMETHING THAT YOU ALREADY BELIEVE TO BE TRUE.

"Later on, you may want to study imagery, which is forming pictures of success in the mind, but that's a little deeper than we want to go right now.

"For the time being, you can use the 'Yes, But...Theory' and, for all practical purposes, get the same results, and it's much simpler."

"Would you suggest a statement I could make?"

"Sure. Just remember that it must be something you believe."

John laughed. "I believe I'm in a batting slump," he joked.

Coach Smith laughed with him. "Yes," he said. "You believe it, but it isn't positive. You must have something that will generate good feelings."

I admired Coach Smith's style. What had been a serious and frustrating condition, now had a relaxed atmosphere with both of them laughing about it.

"I hope I can do that when I become a coach," I thought.

The coach said, "What about saying something like, 'I'm a .350 hitter' before each swing? That's the truth and is a positive thought.

"Also, this may be a good place to use the 'Yes, But...Theory' and say something like, 'Yes, I'm in a batting slump, but it's only temporary and will soon pass'."

"That sounds good. I'll do it. Thanks, Coach," John said eagerly as he turned and signaled his partner that he was ready for more pitches.

Coach Smith turned without watching John take any swings, and walked toward another group of players. He didn't seem overly-concerned about John's hitting.

I wondered if this was because he thought John's batting slump was about to end, or if he just wanted to show John he had confidence in him.

Coach Norman motioned for us to move away from the batting cage.

"Do any of you have a question about self-talk?" he asked.

Very quickly, Sam spoke, "I don't have questions about self-talk, Coach, but we've heard the 'Yes, But...Theory' mentioned again. When are we going to hear about it?"

"Boy! You've sure developed an interest in it, haven't you?" Coach Norman said laughing and slapping Sam on the shoulder.

"I sure have!"

"Good. That's one of our favorite ways of teaching the mental game, and I think it's about time to get into it.

"Before presenting it to you, though, I wanted to make sure you understood three things.

"One, the mind and body work together to create good play. Two, the mental picture. And three, for self-talk to be positive, it must be something we actually believe to be true."

He looked at his watch and said, "Let's go over to the science department. It's about time for them to conduct an experiment I think will be helpful to you in understanding the 'Yes, But...Theory'."

Sam and I looked at each other, wondering the same thing— 'How can a science experiment help us understand a coaching philosophy?'

4.
The 'Yes, But... Theory'

Winners aim at what is out of sight for a loser.

Entering the building, we walked down the hallway to a classroom. The sign over the door read, SCIENCE ROOM, MR. JAMES SCRIBNER.

Coach Norman motioned for us to gather around him. "There are two things I want you to watch. First, I want you to notice the students' attitudes during the experiment. Second, notice how they act immediately after the experiment is over.

He tapped lightly on the large, glass pane in the door to get Mr. Scribner's attention, who looked up and motioned for us to enter.

"Mr. Scribner," Coach said, "this is Dean, Sam, Marc and Richie. They're here from the University to tour our school and would like to watch your science experiment."

"Certainly," the teacher said. "Welcome to our classroom.

"We're about ready to begin," he said as he turned and walked to a desk where several students were standing in a semi-circle on the opposite side.

"The experiment will be conducted here," he told us. "If you will stand behind me, you'll have a good view."

He opened the doors under the desk and removed a round glass dish, about eight inches across and an inch deep.

He set two containers, one about a gallon; one much smaller, on the desktop.

THE SCIENCE EXPERIMENT

"What we're going to do," he explained, "is take a strong acid and neutralize it with another chemical. By neutralizing, I mean we will render a dangerous acid harmless."

He picked up the large container. "This is hydrochloric acid. It's highly corrosive and has a variety of uses.

"It's so strong, industry sometimes uses it to clean metal."

He let his eyes pass over all the students and sternly said, "I want you to pay attention and be very careful. There is to be no horseplay. If these chemicals should get on you, you could be severely burned. In fact, they are both lethal."

"What does lethal mean?" one girl asked.

There was a hint of a smile on the science teacher's face as he said, "It means they could cause death!"

That was enough warning. All stood motionless with solemn expressions. Their eyes were all fixed either on the chemicals or the teacher.

As he poured the hydrochloric acid into the dish, a strong odor began to fill the room. The students' apprehension increased as the experiment progressed and the odor gained strength.

Proceeding, the teacher said, "This is a strong and dangerous acid, but after we neutralize it, it will be little more than tap water."

He picked up the smaller container filled with a white flaky substance. I saw the words 'sodium hydroxide' written on it.

When he began putting it into the acid, we all inched backward, leery of what might happen. We held our breath, but, to our surprise, there was no noticeable reaction.

"Is that it?" one girl asked.

"I think so," he said and placed his hand about an inch above the mixture.

"Oh, be careful, Mr. Scribner!" the girl begged.

"There's no reason to be afraid of it now. I could wash my hands in what was a dangerous acid."

All the students looked at him, trying to decide if he really meant what he had said.

"Are you sure?" one asked.

"I'm positive. It's no longer harmful. Its only salt water now," he said putting his four fingers into the mixture sloshing it around.

The 'Yes, But... Theory' 31

As Coach Norman had requested, I looked at the students.

Everyone began to relax. Some had to take long, deep breaths to release their tension, but all evidence of nervousness quickly disappeared.

Some began talking with their friends, and one boy actually turned and leaned against the table with his backside near the dish. None were looking at the dish which only a minute earlier had, almost hypnotically, held their attention.

I looked at the coach. He was smiling as if to say, "I knew what the reaction would be."

"Thanks, Mr. Scribner," he said, and nodded his head toward the door, letting us know it was time to leave.

Richie and I were the first to enter the hallway. I quietly whispered to him, "What did that have to do with mental training?"

He held out his hands palm up and shrugged his shoulders, but dropped them as the coach came out the door.

The coach led us out to a pavilion with several benches. He invited us to sit and selected a bench facing us.

Smiling mischievously, he said, "That was an interesting experiment, wasn't it?"

He knew we were confused, and just sat there for awhile saying nothing—teasing us with his silence.

Careful not to carry the joke too far, he quickly became serious and sympathized with us.

"I know it's unclear to you how the science class is related to our 'Yes, But...Theory', but just be patient and I'll explain. I promise it will help you understand our mental training philosophy."

The coach then became even more serious. He leaned forward, putting his elbows on his knees. It was as if he were trying to get closer to make sure we heard him.

"Don't you find it interesting how something so strong can be neutralized and lose its power almost immediately? How something can create enough fear to hold an entire class breathless one minute and become so weak it's almost forgotten the next?"

He didn't wait for us to answer.

"Wouldn't it be great if we could find a way to neutralize all those things that smudge our mental picture?" he said as he waved his hand from one side to the other as if there were things all around ready to attack our self-image.

He was asking questions, but we knew he wasn't wanting an answer.

"Imagine yourself to be John, the hitter we just saw in the batting cage. If you were facing a batting slump, wouldn't it be great if we could pour a solution on it and take away all its power to disrupt?

"Take Bill, the golfer. Think how nice it would be if, when he muffed the shot, we could sprinkle on a neutralizer that would insure no harm would come to his mental image?"

"That would be super!" Richie said.

The coach nodded. "It sure would. If we could do that, then the good that happens to us would build our confidence and we could prevent the bad experiences from tearing us down."

CONFIDENCE

One of the keys to success is confidence.

No team or individual can play their best while shouldering lack of confidence.

Whether it 'just happened' or was planned, all who are successful have devised a way of letting favorable experiences increase their confidence, but won't let unfavorable experiences tear them down.

Not even natural talent can be rated above this in striving for success.

Coach Norman rose from his bench, placed his hands together in front of him and slowly rubbed his palms together. I could tell he was gathering his thoughts as he moved about in front of us. His actions and tone of voice were no longer that of a person carrying on a casual conversation, but resembled a professor beginning to lecture on an important subject.

"You have all shown an interest in our 'Yes, But...Theory' of mental training," he said, speaking deliberately. "But I have intentionally held off discussing it with you until you became aware of those other things we talked about.

"First, I wanted to make sure you realize the mind has an influence on how we perform physically.

"Second, I wanted you to know we have a mental picture of ourselves in our mind—an image which is formed by what we tell ourselves.

"Also, I wanted you to know that only what we believe to be true will affect our self-image. If we consider anything to be untrue, it has no effect on us.

"I wanted you to observe the science experiment because its goal and method resembles our 'Theory'.

"Just like the acid, we want to neutralize those things which are harmful to performance.

"To show a comparison between the experiment and our 'Theory', let's begin with the acid.

FEARS WON'T LEAVE ON THEIR OWN

"The classroom was no longer normal once Mr. Scribner placed the acid into the dish. There was fear and apprehension everywhere.

"I'm not making fun of, or laughing at the students. Their fear was justified. The acid could have ruined their clothing, burned their skin, blinded them or even caused death. There were plenty of reasons to fear it.

"It would have been poor judgment to have said, 'Oh, don't worry about it, it will eventually dissolve and be gone'.

"Normal classroom activity could never return until something was done with the acid.

"Negatives have the same effect on our performance.

"Until we deal with the negatives, normal performance is out of the question.

"Doubts, fears, slumps and lack of confidence cause just as much chaos and turmoil in our 'performing lives' as the acid did in the classroom.

"And, just as the fear in the classroom was justified, so are the dangers we imagine when negatives creep into our thoughts.

"They can lead to unhappiness, poor performance, loss of our position on the team, and at the extreme, be fatal to our careers—we may give up and quit.

"Yes, there is reason to be frightened of negatives.

"It would be just as ridiculous to say, 'Don't worry about them and they will eventually go away and normalcy will return,' as it would be to wait for the acid to evaporate.

"For normal performance to return, something must be done with the negatives.

Coach Norman paused, walked back to his bench, and sat down.

None of us spoke, completely engrossed in what he had been saying.

"This is good stuff!" I thought. I had always considered coaching to be only teaching fundamentals and getting players in good physical condition. I never realized how important it was to get the mind in order.

"Do you understand this comparison of the acid in the classroom and the negatives in our mind?" he asked.

"I think I do," I said. "Both the acid and negatives create justifiable fear and must be dealt with before productive activity can return. Also, we can't just ignore them and they will go away."

"That's right," Coach agreed. "But remember, fear is the key word.

"If we are afraid we will 'miss a shot', 'strike out', 'be cut from the squad', 'lose a game' or 'fail in anyway', we cannot perform normally.

"To perform well, fear must be eliminated.

"If fear is present, we will be apprehensive, filled with anxiety and effective behavior may vanish.

"If we can rid ourselves of doubt and fear, we will also rid ourselves of anxieties and apprehensions, and stand a much better chance of performing effectively."

REMOVING THE THREAT REMOVES THE FEAR

"Coach Norman," Dean asked, "isn't it impossible to remove fear? If we are afraid of something, we fear it, and that's it, isn't it?"

"It's easy to see why you would feel this way, Dean," he said, "but, that's not necessarily so.

"Many coaches feel as you do and fail to help their young players remove their fears. Actually, many coaches, by their coaching methods, increase or create fears within their players' minds. This is a very, very serious mistake.

The 'Yes, But... Theory' 35

"Let me give you a couple of examples of how fear can be removed.

"If you were being chased by an angry, wild animal, your fear would be great. But if an animal control officer shot it with a tranquilizer gun and the animal went to sleep, your fears would almost completely disappear. Why? Because the animal no longer has the capacity to harm you. The animal is still there, but it can no longer harm you, so you no longer fear it.

"Suppose you were in the midst of a raging storm. You would be very fearful. Once you enter an adequate storm shelter, your fear will lessen considerably. The storm is still there, but it can't reach you, so you're not nearly as anxious. You may be afraid some property may be damaged, but for your own well-being, the fear is gone.

"Fear can be removed.

"Without the power to harm, fear vanishes."

ADMIT A PROBLEM EXISTS

"I'm sure all of you can see that the next step in our analogy of the science experiment and our mental training is 'how to rid ourselves of fear'.

"The first step in eliminating fear is to point it out to ourselves.

"The first thing Mr. Scribner did in the experiment was admit there was a danger. He told them 'it's caustic', 'it can burn', 'it can blind' and 'it can kill.'

"It would have been poor judgment to have tried to deny a danger existed. To do so, could have resulted in serious injury.

"Can't you imagine a classroom full of students moving around saying 'There's nothing in here that will harm me', and all the while looking over their shoulder to make sure no one was fooling around with the acid?

"Denying a fear you know is real won't bring normal actions.

"The same holds true in athletics. If a player is in a hitting slump, shooting percentages down, a tight end is dropping catchable balls, or a golfer is slicing the ball, it is fruitless to deny the problem exists.

"Its not only useless, it can be damaging. SAYING one thing, but BELIEVING the opposite can lead to inner conflict. Few things can be more damaging to players' effectiveness than conflict within themselves.

"It isn't soothing to a baseball player in a slump to say, 'I'm hitting the ball well', when he knows he has only one hit in his last 15 at-bats.

"A basketball player who is shooting poorly can find no rest by saying,

We all have problems and it's important how we approach them. Problems must be admitted, not denied. When we admit our problems exist we can develop a plan to overcome them. Failing to admit problems won't take away the influence they will have on us.

The "Yes, But... Theory"

'I'm a good shooter', when he actually feels he is having trouble even hitting lay-ups.

"A golfer who continually finds himself in the rough due to his slice, but tells himself he is hitting the ball straight, is only increasing his anxiety. And, anxiety and good smooth play just don't travel together.

THE "YES" OF THE "YES, BUT...THEORY"

"You can't erase a fear by denying it exists.

"This is the 'Yes' of our 'Yes, But...Theory'.

"If there is a problem, admit it. Say, 'yes, I'm in a batting slump', 'yes, I'm shooting poorly' or 'yes, my tennis serve is erratic'.

"There are two reasons players should admit a negative.

"First, it stops any internal conflict. It avoids saying one thing while thinking another.

"Second, and maybe more important, it gets the problem out in the open where it can be attacked. If we admit it is there, then a plan can be developed to remedy it.

"If we deny it exists, then, to us, there is nothing to correct. We can't attack something that isn't there.

"It would be like an army that says 'We have no enemies, but we are off to battle our foes. If there are no enemies, there is no one to battle.

"If a player says, 'I have no problem', there is nothing to solve.

"Only after its existence is admitted can a plan of correction be developed.

"We cannot remove a fear or doubt until we admit we are afraid or doubtful.

DON'T DENY FEAR—ATTACK IT

"The solution is admit and attack!

"Challenging the negative is important. Whether junior high or professional, players who are allowed to harbor negatives over a period of time may get caught up in the 'circle of failure'."

Anticipating our question, Coach said, "It is called the circle of failure because negatives lead to worry, worry to fear, fear to tension and tension to poor performance. Poor performance leads to more negatives, and the cycle goes on and on.

"The cycle must be broken or it will continue to increase until it completely dominates the player.

"Many players try to stop it by concentrating on the negative. They try to push it out of their mind—forget it—don't think about it, but it doesn't work. The negative is still there, it still has the same meaning to them, and continues to create fear.

"At Chaucer, we try to stop the cycle by attacking 'fear'.

"We use the same principle the science teacher used to stop the fear associated with the acid. He used another chemical to neutralize it—he took away its capacity to harm. I'm going to show you how we use a positive to take away the threat created by a negative.

"With no threat, there is no fear."

FEAR REDUCING PRINCIPLES

"To understand how to do this, there are two things you must know.

"One, the mind can only hold one thought at a time.

"The mind may switch at lightning speed from one thought to another, but it can only think of one thing at a time.

"The second thing you need to know is 'the mind will concentrate on the most important element'.

"We use these two principles to neutralize negatives.

"To help me explain this, think back to the science experiment.

"When we were about to enter the science room, I told you to notice the students' attitudes during the experiment and also, immediately afterwards.

"Did you notice their attitudes while the acid was in its original state?" he asked, waiting for an answer.

"I did," Sam spoke up. "They didn't move, speak, and they kept their eyes glued to it."

"They gave it their complete attention, right?" the coach asked.

Sam nodded his head in agreement.

"Why do you think they acted that way, Sam?"

"After the teacher told them what it could do, they were afraid of it!"

"Right," the coach said. "They felt threatened. The fear of the acid captured all their attention.

The 'Yes, But... Theory' 39

"Acid was their one thought. Why? It was the most important to them. The dangers the acid posed to them overrode all other possible thoughts in their minds.

"So, the mind had one thought—the acid. The reason—it was the most important."

FOCUSING ON FEAR HURTS PERFORMANCE

"Athletics is no different. We fear anything that can hurt our performance.

"When we have doubts, make mistakes, go into slumps, or any of the many things that can smudge our mental picture, we're afraid.

"If it can harm us, we fear it, and, as a result, we focus on it more.

"When we focus on negatives, our performance suffers.

"Earlier, I said our thoughts may switch from one thing to another, but the most important idea will be the most dominate. Now what could be more important to us than fear?"

The four of us looked at each other blankly.

The coach continued, "All human beings have an instinctive desire for survival. When that's threatened, all senses focus on the threat.

"The same thing may very well happen when we feel our survival as an athlete is in jeopardy."

NEUTRALIZED FEARS WILL DISAPPEAR

"Now think back to the science experiment. Once Mr. Scribner had neutralized the acid and told the class it was nothing but salt water, what happened?"

I remembered the nonchalant attitude they had and I said, "They completely ignored the dish. They turned their back to it, some visited with other students, and one boy almost sat in it."

"Yes," he said. "their concentration left it."

"At first, the acid was the most important thing to them and it dominated their thoughts. When it became unimportant, it was forgotten.

"They concentrated on the most important.

"With the fear gone, the acid wasn't the most important.

"In our mental training, we try to do the same thing—remove the fear by neutralizing the negative.

"Mr. Scribner used another chemical as a neutralizer.

"You'll see we can neutralize a negative withw a positive.

'BUT' OF THE 'YES, BUT...THEORY'

"Using a positive to neutralize the negative is the 'But' of our 'Yes, But...Theory'.

"The word 'but' can be very powerful. It's not quite like the word 'not' which changes a statement from positive to negative, but it can greatly alter the importance of an idea.

"To make a point, Marc, suppose your coach walked up to you and told you, 'I'm going to start you in center field today in the big game'. How would you feel?"

"I'd feel great! Excited!"

"Sure you would," he replied. "But, suppose he came to you and said, 'Marc, I'm going to start you in center field today, but...', and then he was interrupted and never finished the sentence. How would you feel? Would you be as excited?"

"I probably wouldn't," I said. "I would be wondering what he meant by 'but'..."

He smiled and said, "Yes, the word 'but' changed the importance of it, didn't it?"

He turned to Richie and said, "Richie, let's assume the homecoming queen at the University sent you a note which read, 'Richie, I will go to the Homecoming Dance with you'. Would this excite you?"

"Of course!"

"Yes," the coach said grinning, "you would probably want to get new clothes, get your hair trimmed, and make all kinds of plans.

"But, suppose you received a note which read, "Richie, I will go to the Homecoming Dance with you, but...', and the rest of the note had been smudged and you couldn't read it? Would the note be as exciting?"

"Probably not," Richie admitted.

"You see," he said, "the word 'but' can be real powerful. When used this way it takes much of the importance away from the statement that preceded it.

"Earlier, I told you the 'Yes' of the Theory was to admit the problem.

"Sam, suppose you have been having trouble with your freethrows, and you said, 'Yes, my freethrows have been poor'. This sounds bad. It's discouraging—even frightening.

"Let's change the statement and say, 'Yes, I've been having trouble with my freethrows, but...'. This sounds better, doesn't it? By just saying 'but' it took part of the importance away from the statement.

"Although nothing has been specifically stated, it indicates to us something is going to be said that will downplay the fact you are not shooting freethrows well.

"The word 'but' makes you feel that for some reason or another things aren't too bad."

GIVE THE MIND A CHOICE BETWEEN TWO THOUGHTS: THE PROBLEM AND A GOOD THOUGHT

"Imagine how it would sound if we put a statement after 'but' that gave proof shooting was not such a big deal.

"'My freethrow shooting is poor', is a scary statement.

"'My freethrow shooting is poor, but...', isn't quite so frightening.

"'My freethrow shooting is poor, but, I have a sprained wrist which is about healed, and I probably will be back to normal', creates little, if any, fear.

"Remember, the mind can only hold one thought at a time and will concentrate on the most important.

"In the first statement, poor freethrow shooting is the only thought, so it's what the mind will hold. Since it causes fear, normal playing probably won't happen.

"In the last statement, 'healed wrist' and 'a good possibility of returning to normal' are the most important thoughts, and will dominate the mind. There is no fear associated with this thought, therefore, normal activity will probably prevail.

"Let's review the process of stopping the negative influence of a personal athletic problem.

"A problem is threatening and causes fear.

"Fear is important, and because we concentrate on the most important, it becomes our main thought. This makes normal performance nearly impossible.

"Denying a problem exists won't dissolve it. Also, a plan of attack can't be formulated until a problem is admitted.

"To quit emphasizing a problem, it must be degraded to at least 'second place' in importance.

"We degrade it by admitting it exists and following the admission with 'but' and a more important positive.

"This causes the mind to concentrate on the positive rather than the problem.

"The 'Yes, But...Theory' resembles holding up two flash cards to the mind's eye. Able to pick only one, it will pick the most important.

"We present two ideas to our thought process. One is a negative and one a positive. If the positive is the most important, the mind will dwell on it.

"Thinking positively encourages smooth and effective play, and also, brings improvement.?"

SUMMARY

To be successful, a player must be at ease with himself and pleased with the existing situation.

This is not possible with doubt, fear, and apprehension present.

The first step in ridding oneself of these negatives, is to admit a problem exists. This will do two things for the athlete:

1. It avoids internal conflict. It will insure the mind is not being pulled in two directions.

2. It gets the problem out in the open where a plan to defeat it can be developed.

Fear is the greatest adversary of smooth effective play. It must be erased from the mind.

Fear comes from a feeling of being threatened. If the threat can be eliminated, fear will be removed.

To eliminate a threat, the mind must concentrate on something positive.

In order for the mind to 'choose' to dwell on a positive rather than a negative, the positive must carry more importance to the player than the negative.

This is possible because:

1. The mind can only think of one idea at a time.

2. The mind will concentrate on the idea that is the most important.

3. Almost all situations have a positive that is more important than the

The 'Yes, But... Theory' 43

negative.

The player can change from negative to positive dominated thinking by admitting (YES) a problem exists (BUT) and inserting a positive thought that is more important than the negative.

5.
Just Forget It??

For the shortest route to
failure, take the "fear" exit.

John was back in the batting cage when we returned to the baseball field.

He wasn't talking to himself anymore. At least, not out loud, but he was smashing the ball.

Earlier, he had been hitting on top of the ball, creating slow rollers or getting under the ball popping it up, but now he was hitting balls which would be linedrives, hard grounders and maybe homeruns.

I wished I could tell if he were silently using the "Yes, But...Theory'. I bet he was. Anyway, it appeared his slump may be coming to an end.

Sam walked closer to the cage and intently watched John's hitting. Richie and Dean glanced at each other, exchanging smiles. They knew Sam was doing some serious thinking.

CAN'T WE FORGET?

He let us know his thoughts when he turned to Coach Norman and asked, "Why couldn't a coach just tell John to forget about the slump? If he would do that, the effect would go away, wouldn't it?"

The coach gave Sam the same good-natured smile we had been seeing all morning. "You're right, Sam. If he could forget the slump, the influence probably would go away. That would be good advice except for one thing—forgetting can be extremely difficult.

"Do you see Bob, the boy working out on third base? Watch him throw the ball."

We all turned and watched Bob field balls a coach was hitting to him. His throws to first base were strong and accurate, and he got rid of the ball quickly when throwing to second base to start a double play.

It didn't take long to see he was a good third baseman.

"Whew!" Richie exclaimed. "He looks like college material."

"He is," the coach affirmed. "Bob is the best in the league at that position. One of his strongest points is his arm, but early in the season his arm became very erratic. He struggled with it, but the more he tried to work it out, the worse it became.

"We had a new assistant coach who had never had our ideas on mental training explained to him. The coach knew the root of Bob's problem was mental. He realized Bob still was physically capable of making good throws, but had allowed negative thoughts to work their way into his mind, disrupting his performance.

"Not fully understanding what would happen, he suggested Bob just forget it. 'Once you get the throwing slump out of your mind and forget it, your good form will return,' he told him.

"Bob is a very dedicated player and has confidence in the coaching staff. He believed the coach and set out to rid his mind of the problem.

"The coach was right. If a negative can be forgotten, the influence will end, but forgetting isn't always easy.

TRYING TO FORGET CAN BE FRUSTRATING

"Bob soon realized he had a problem he couldn't handle. To forget something using conscious effort is impossible.

"He found forgetting means not knowing it exists. It must be completely out of your mind. Every time he consciously tried to forget, he was reminding himself of the situation.

"Every time he would think, 'I'm going to forget my poor throw', 'poor throw' was the main thought in his mind. The more he tried to forget, the more he was reminding himself of the condition."

"But, we do forget things in our life, don't we?" Richie asked. "I've forgotten many things. How did that happen?"

"We forget that which is not really important to us," the coach told him.

"If this had been one of those everyday problems we all run into, he would

Just Forget It??   47

probably have forgotten it before the day was over, but this was serious to him. It bothered him that he was hurting the team's chances of winning, and also, it was jeopardizing the starting position he once had a strong hold on.

"It was important, so, he was constantly reminding himself of it. Since he was reminding himself, he was unable to forget."

"Oh. Okay, I can see that," Richie admitted.

Coach continued with his explanation. "When he found he not only couldn't forget it, but it actually was getting stronger in his mind, it compounded his problem. He became more anxious, and as a result, his throw got worse rather than better."

The strong, accurate throws Bob was making were proof to Sam the problem had been settled.

"What did he do, and how long did it take him to correct his poor throw?"

We were astonished by the coach's answer. "Once he put it in the correct perspective, about a day and a half."

Our expressions of surprise caused a smile to spread across his face.

PRINCIPLES OF THE THEORY

"Now," he teased, "let's see what kind of students you are? Let me give you a little test. I said he settled his problem once he put it in the correct perspective. What do you think Bob had to do?"

Sam was the first to offer an answer. "Since the mind can only think of one thing at a time, he kept thinking about something good and didn't allow the negative to enter his thoughts."

"You're partially right," the coach agreed. But, remember, this problem was serious to him and it would have been difficult for him to keep the negative from pushing the positive aside and returning to his thoughts."

"Somehow he had to lessen the importance of the negative," Dean suggested.

"All right," Coach Norman said happily. "You are both pretty good students. Both of you deserve a passing grade on the test, but you need to combine your answers into one.

"Sam, you're right, the mind can only think of one thing at a time, and if we can think of a positive rather than a negative, it will solve the problem. There is one thing, however, you must never forget—we concentrate on that which is the most important. As Dean said, the positive must be the most important to Bob.

"In importance, the positive must outweigh the negative."

"Also, it must be factual," Richie reminded him.

"Yes," Coach said, "if we don't consider it to be a fact, we won't think it's more important and will still concentrate on the problem.

"Think back to the acid neutralizing demonstration. The negative, like the acid, must be put into a position where it will not cause any fear. If we don't fear it, we won't be so apt to focus on it.

"In the demonstration, the fear was removed by neutralizing it with another chemical. It was changed from acid to salt water. No one was afraid of salt water so their thoughts turned to other things.

"Bob's 'acid', a wild throw, needed to be neutralized by a positive he considered more important to him than the wildness of his throw; something that would attract his attention more than the throwing problem.

"Decreasing the importance will decrease the fear.

"Decreasing fear decreases the influence it has on our performance.

"When Bob tried to forget, he was trying to dissolve his thoughts while they were still important to him. This only increased his problems.

"He became more anxious when he couldn't forget. Conflicting thoughts like 'I'm going to forget—but, I'm not forgetting' also increased his anxiety.

"Trying to remove a thought from the mind using conscious effort can be frustrating. It's perplexing because it's impossible.

"Think of the anxiety that would have been created if Mr. Scribner had tried to remove the shallow dish with the acid in its original form. It was much easier to take away its strength.

"The same holds true on worries about our performance. We first must remove the fear associated with them."

NEUTRALIZING A NEGATIVE

Coach Norman explained how Bob's help eventually came from a teammate, Arnie.

One day while Bob was discussing his throw with him, the team's shortstop asked if he had tried the 'Yes, But...Theory' the coach was always talking about.

Bob admitted he hadn't, but said he was so frustrated he was ready to try anything.

Just Forget It?? 49

Bob asked, "Would you help me formulate an appropriate statement?"

"According to Coach's theory," Arnie pointed out, "we need a positive statement that is true. We can't lie to ourselves and do any good. Also, the statement must hold more importance to you than your poor throwing."

Bob was unable to think of anything. At the moment, nothing seemed more important to him than his terrible throws.

It was Arnie who came up with the solution.

"Bob," he said, "if your arm was broken and in a cast, and the doctor said you were going to be out for the season, I would be especially concerned. But I know there is nothing physically wrong with the arm, and it's the best of any third baseman in the league.

"Also, I know the season is a long way from being over and this problem you are having is only temporary. We both know it will soon pass.

"You have made our team very solid at that corner of the diamond, and I know you will make it solid again. That's what's important to me. Not the fact you're going through a temporary slump.

"I hate to see you troubled with this, but we all have setbacks along the way. In all probability it will make you a better player in the future if you handle it correctly."

The neutralizing statement they came up with was, 'Yes, I'm having trouble with my throws, but physically and fundamentally I have one of the best arms in the area. I still have the physical capabilities. I haven't lost them. The only problem I have is my mind is interfering with my body in the performance of the fundamentals. This is only temporary and will soon pass. I have been over-reacting to a not-so-great problem'.

The thought, 'I have one of the best arms of the area' made salt water out of his problem almost as quickly as the chemical did in the acid demonstration.

SUMMARY

- ✔ To forget something that is troubling us can be difficult.
- ✔ To forget something using conscious effort is impossible.
- ✔ We forget that which is unimportant.

6.
Will It Always Work?

Many losses occur because defeat is admitted before it happens.

There wasn't a doubt in my mind this theory was an effective way to train young players, but one question kept coming to my mind.

I approached the coach with it.

ARE SOME PROBLEMS TOO LARGE FOR THIS 'THEORY'?

"Are there problems so large you couldn't find a positive with more importance than the negative?"

"Yes, Marc, that's a good question," he said. "You can find such situations, but seldom.

"That's one of the first questions asked when I explain our method.

"Since it's one of the first things that comes to people's minds when we discuss the 'Theory', it points to a great misconception in mental training. All of us seem to have a natural tendency to 'think big' when thinking about the mental game.

"The truth is, most athletes go through their entire career without running into a problem that can't be neutralized."

SUCCESS ATTITUDES ARE BUILT ON SMALL THINGS

"Most successes and failures are not determined by serious happenings. It is rare when you can put a finger on a particular reason why one individual or team became a consistent winner or why another continually struggled."

He looked at me and said, "I'm sure you have several friends, don't you?"

"Well..., I think so," I hesitated.

"Think of one particular friend, and tell me why the two of you became friends."

I thought for a few seconds "I really don't know. We just like one another. We just naturally hit it off, I guess."

"It's hard to pinpoint the reason, isn't it?"

I nodded.

He continued, "Success and failure attitudes are like friendships—they are developed over a long period of time. Friendships are based on a myriad of happenings, situations, words spoken and words not spoken.

"We become friends because of day-to-day, positive experiences. If these experiences become negative, then the friendship will die.

"Athletics is no different. Positive thoughts and experiences lead to winning attitudes and negatives lead to losing ones. Most are developed because of the way the player reacted to everyday small situations and experiences, not by big catastrophic failures or successes.

"Just as friendships don't happen because someone gave us a million dollars, winning attitudes don't develop because we hit a homerun in the bottom of the last inning to win a championship.

"Friendships grow. So do winning attitudes.

"No friendly relationship is without negatives. If the world's best friendship was carefully scrutinized, it would be found that both parties have traits the other considers negative. But, these don't affect the friendship. Why? Because each side has chosen to think on the goodness of the other, rather than the negatives.

"Winning attitudes grow and maintain themselves the same way.

"Everyone continually encounters small negatives, but the winner has learned to place a positive as their focal point. They have learned to say 'Yes, But...', and let the positive move to the front of their thoughts."

SMALL PROBLEMS NEED ATTENTION, TOO

I asked, "Are you saying we should deal with the small and forget the large?"

"No. No. That's definitely not what I'm saying," he said quickly. "What I'm saying is that most of the average careers are determined by small things. This happens because there just aren't that many large problems.

"Every problem a player meets, whether large or small, should be dealt with to the best of our ability.

"The problem is, most mental training effort is directed toward big problems. Since there aren't many of these, there isn't much mental training going on.

"There are very few major situations, but small things are happening continually. These, too, need to be counteracted. This counteraction can come from the player himself, the coach or both. One thing is for certain, it needs to be done on a regular basis.

"Most players need to reassure themselves, or be reassured by the coach, after a missed lay-up in practice, a bad-hop error in baseball, a missed blocking assignment in football, or failure to get a serve over the net in tennis.

"These things, and thousands of others like them, if not handled properly, can build up until confidence is shaken, doubt creeps in, or capabilities are questioned.

"Coaches deal with the glaring emotional problems and fail to see such things as the boy or girl who has developed a misguided opinion that successful athletes never make a mistake. To these youngsters, every mistake is a failure, and every mistake they make siphons off a little more of their confidence.

"Just a little explanation about the reality of life—everyone, even the pros, make mistakes—and a small neutralizing statement could turn a potential disaster into a success. A tag-along-with-the-team player may be changed into one who will make the team stronger."

Dean asked, "What kind of neutralizing statement would you give a player like this?"

Without much thought, the coach said, "A good statement would be 'Yes, I make mistakes, but, that's normal. Everyone makes mistakes. I will practice hard to limit my mistakes to as few as possible, but when I make one, I will know it isn't a sign of failure'."

The coach looked at each of us to see if there were other questions, and then continued, "Anyone interested in mental training should be aware that a player doesn't have to come apart at the seams before his performance is affected. A small, depressing situation can spoil peak performance, and anything 'less than best' reduces the chances of success for the player as well as the team.

PLAYERS HAVE NO CONTROL OVER SOME PROBLEMS

"Success in many careers has been interrupted by little things the player has no control over.

"I remember a pitcher," he said, "who, after three games, had an earned run average of 1.5, but had not won a game. Although he had pitched well, this had the potential to be very discouraging.

"If not handled properly, he could start pressing, trying harder, or become disgruntled at the other players for not scoring more runs.

"It wasn't his fault, it wasn't major, and he had been pitching well, but there was a possibility his entire season could be disrupted.

"A good statement for him to make would be, 'Yes, I am 0-3, but I have pitched just like I hoped I would. I have no control over how many runs our team scores. Possibly, in some future game, the team will score enough runs to win when I don't pitch as well. It will probably balance out before the season is over. I'm happy with the way I've pitched."

We sat for awhile discussing various situations and conditions, real and hypothetical. Coach Norman was his usual self in answering our questions.

I suppose the coach was right about us wanting to think big, because our conversation returned to major situations.

He explained, "Yes, there are a few situations where it would be hard to find a positive that's more important than the negative you're facing. They are few and far between and most players will never encounter one of them.

USE OF THE 'THEORY' DEVELOPS POSITIVE ATTITUDES

"It would be a poor excuse to not use the 'Yes, But...Theory' on the

Will It Always Work? 55

thousands of situations where it will work, just because there are a few problems a statement won't neutralize.

"Once a player becomes accustomed to using the Theory in incidental situations, a positive approach to problems will happen without thought.

"Should the player be faced with a crisis, the automatic positive-thinking mechanism he has built into his life will 'kick-in' to support him through the problem.

"So, although there are problems so large you may be unable to find a neutralizing statement, the 'Theory' will still give you indirect help. The positive attitude which will be developed by using it in small situations will aid you in getting through any crisis."

SUMMARY

There could be some problems too large for a counteracting positive statement to be found.

This shouldn't be discouraging, because:

1. Careers are based on how everyday small problems are handled.

2. Most players never have a major crisis in their entire career.

3. If a crisis should arise, the attitude developed by using the 'Theory' in small things will help carry a player through the major problem.

7.
The Trojan Horse

When there is more vision than television, chances for success increase.

We had seen two baseball players attempt to end slumps using the 'Yes, But...Theory'. One slump affected the arm; the other, the bat.

These were interesting, but I wished I could see an example of the 'Theory' being used on some small everyday problem.

Talkative Dean took care of my wishes.

Leaving the baseball field, we entered the gym through the rear door. Dean stopped when he saw a sign over a dressing room door which read, 'Make your attitude toward practice positive'. The word 'make' had been underlined.

"Boy!" he said, "The coach who put that sign up would have been mad at me yesterday."

"Why do you say that?" the coach quizzed him.

"Oh, I don't know why, but I just didn't want to go to practice yesterday," he said.

"Were you ill?" the coach continued questioning him.

"No. I wasn't sick. I just wasn't into practice, I guess."

"Let's sit here on the bleachers for a while," Coach Norman suggested. "This brings up a good point in mental training."

Sam, Richie and I looked at Dean and smiled. He knew what we were thinking. Oh, boy, Dean. Your mouth has gotten you in trouble again.

Dean sat as far away from the coach as he could. We could tell he was wishing he had never mentioned the sign.

EVERYONE HAS NEGATIVE FEELINGS

"Dean," the coach said, leaning forward, peering around the rest of us to see Dean on the other end of the bleacher. "Your feelings were no different than anyone else's.

"There has never been a player or coach who has not, at one time or another, dreaded going to practice.?"

Dean began to relax, but I admit I had a little twinge of disappointment because Coach Norman didn't drag him 'through the fire' a little before letting him up. I should have known better. Coach Norman just wasn't that type person.

"All of us have gone to practice wishing we didn't have to go. We would much rather be doing something other than working on fundamentals for two hours," he continued.

"But, think about this: Would you consider this feeling to be negative?"

Dean had a sheepish smile. "Well, you sure couldn't consider it to be positive, could you?"

"No," he said. "Though we're all guilty of doing this occasionally, I would still have to rate it a negative, and negatives and peak performance just don't travel in the same buggy, do they?"

I had been waiting to see the 'Theory' applied to an everyday problem, and here it was. "Would you use the 'Theory' in this situation?" I asked eagerly.

"Definitely. We don't consider any negative too small to be ignored.

"Our attitude at Chaucer is, 'if you take care of the little problems, most of the large ones will never occur'.

"Allowing little negatives to go unchallenged can be compared to the Trojan Horse.

"You remember the story of the Wooden Horse of Troy, and how the invading army was unable to overthrow a city because of the strong walls surrounding it.

"They built a large, wooden horse, and hid a few soldiers inside. They pulled it to the city gates and offered it as a gift.

"When the army left, the people of the city opened their gates, pulled the horse inside and closed the gates.

"When night fell, the soldiers hiding in the horse slipped out, opened the gates and let the army enter the city.

The Trojan Horse   59

"The city was overthrown because a few insignificant soldiers were allowed to get inside the walls undetected."

"I remember that story from high school English lit," Sam said.

"Me too," Richie added, "and also from history classes."

SMALL UNCHALLENGED NEGATIVES LEAD TO BIG PROBLEMS

The coach continued, "Our minds are like the city behind the walls, and small negatives can be compared to the insignificant soldiers hiding in the wooden horse. If the negatives are allowed to stay in our minds, they will open the door to more and larger problems. The positive outlook in our mind will be overthrown just as the city was.

"We must be alert for any negatives, no matter how small. Just as the soldiers slipped into the city by hiding in the horse, negatives can enter our thoughts unnoticed. They can disguise themselves as small and unimportant, or we may permit them to enter our thoughts because they are masqueraded as something good.

"If we allow the small negatives to stay, they grow, or encourage other bad feelings to enter. Eventually we are trapped in a situation that causes fear and tension.

"When you first think about it, dreading going to practice just one time doesn't seem too bad, does it?" he asked.

I knew Dean didn't want to answer this question, so I spoke up. "Well, without giving it a lot of thought, it doesn't seem too bad."

"We have a Trojan Horse here, don't we?" he asked. "The negatives slipped in undetected."

IMPROVEMENT—THE KEY TO SUCCESS

He asked Sam, "Why do we attend practice?"

Sam's reply was more of a question than an answer. "To get better?"

"Yes, improvement," he said, and to make a point, pushed his closed fist forward into thin air.

"Improvement is one of the most important factors determining whether we win or lose."

> **NOTE**
>
> Success in any activity depends on improvement.
>
> Improvement is our transportation to success. Without it we have no way to get there.
>
> Improvement comes through practice, therefore, practice must be approached with the best possible attitude.
>
> Practice is where games are won and lost. Good practice wins games and poor practice loses them.

"Improvement is our ride to success, and improvement comes in practice. If we attend practice with a negative attitude, what do we have?"

Answering his own question, he said, "We are placing our chance for success in jeopardy."

NEUTRALIZE GUILT FEELINGS

"Gee," Dean said, "I feel guilty!"

"Oh, oh, Dean!" the coach said, standing and good naturedly pointing his finger at him.

Dean was astonished. The puzzled look on his face gave his thoughts away. What have I said now?

"You just let another Trojan Horse filled with soldiers slip by you," he said chuckling.

Dean became even more puzzled.

"I told you negatives would slip passed us into our thoughts appearing either unimportant or as something good.

"You've let two horses in. The first mistake you made was attending practice with a ho-hum attitude. Those negatives didn't seem important, so you did nothing.

"When you expressed guilt, the second horse went by you with the

The Trojan Horse 61

The only way we can reach success is by improvement— steady, continual improvement. It is our transportation to success. Without improvement, we are doomed to fall behind those who are progressing.

negatives dressed as something good.

"At first glance it would appear good that you feel guilty for dreading practice. You may say, 'I feel unhappy for what I did, therefore, I'm paying for my mistake, so I'm making progress'.

"The problem here is, we must have a positive attitude to play our best, and guilt feelings are certainly negative.

"This, too, must be dealt with properly.

"I agree you should be sorry for a mistake, regret you did it and hope you never do it again, but you mustn't carry guilty feelings around with you."

Dean continued to suffer embarrassment and hung his head in bewilderment.

The coach spent a little while kidding Dean to help him get over his uneasiness.

"I don't want to embarrass you, but you just happened to open the door for me to make a couple of points," Coach said. "You really don't mind me picking on you, do you?"

Dean grinned. "No, not really," he said relaxing somewhat.

FORGIVE YOURSELF

The coach went on with his explanation. "Once you are truly regretful about the past mistake, be happy with your present state of mind. Let that be the fuel propelling you forward. Don't let the guilty feelings drag you down like a ball and chain around your leg.

"To borrow a biblical belief, 'repent and be free from guilt'.

"Once you have reached a position of being honestly sorry for something you've done, it's impossible to raise yourself any higher at that moment as far as that incident is concerned. You've done the most you can do. So, be happy and go forward.

This was confusing to me. It seemed one should do more than just be sorry, and I questioned him about it.

He explained, "I said 'at that moment' that was all that could be done. Later, there must be actions leading you the other direction, but at the moment there is nothing else you can do.

"Being sorry and forgiving yourself is the limit, but later, by your actions, you prove your feelings of being sorry."

"Okay, that makes sense," I conceded.

He proceeded, "Have you ever noticed how difficult it is for us to forgive ourselves? We may be quick to forgive even those we are really not fond of, but we will hold on to our own guilt tighter than we would if it were welded upon our shoulders.

"We must forgive ourselves.

"Never hold a grudge against anyone, especially yourself.

"A guilty conscience is a negative."

The coach looked at us, and smiling said, "I see some confused expressions. You're wondering what Dean should have done, correct?"

"Yes!" we all agreed.

"All right," he began, "We have already pointed out that when Dean dreaded going to practice, he shouldn't have ignored it. That would have been a mistake because he would be attending practice with a negative attitude.

"It wouldn't have been good for him to have told himself, 'I really do want to go to practice'. Why? he asked, pointing at Richie.

"He would be either pretending or lying to himself. He wouldn't actually believe it," Richie replied.

Dean again began scrunching down, as if he were trying to disappear into the bleachers.

"Right," the coach agreed, looking at Dean and grinning. "For any statement to be positive, it must be something we feel is true. This would have no effect on his attitude. There is no positive statement here.

"When you tell yourself something you don't feel is true, you stand the chance of developing conflict within yourself. For example, if he said, 'I do want to go to practice', but felt he didn't, it would be conflicting statements and possibly more harmful than the original problem."

Pointing at me, he asked, "What is the first thing Dean needed to do?"

"He must admit a problem exists," I said.

"Yes, admitting it will stop any chance of conflict and get it out in the open where he can plan an attack against it.

"He should say, 'Yes, I dread going to practice, but...', and he stopped there and looked at Dean.

"Dean, since we have sort of embarrassed you in this session, I'm going to let you choose the positive statement that will let you go into practice with a more positive attitude."

Dean was eager to answer this question. With little hesitation, he said,

"Yes, I dread going to practice, but I want to be a winner. To win, I must improve, and the best place to accomplish that is at practice."

"That would be a very good statement," the coach said.

Dean leaned back and smiled. He had dug himself out of another hole.

YOU HAVE A CHOICE

The coach stood and pointed toward the sign over the door and said, "Before we get away from this subject, I want to draw your attention to one more thing about the sign.

"Look at the sign again."

It was a relatively small placard. Written on it in school colors was MAKE YOUR ATTITUDE TOWARD PRACTICE POSITIVE with 'make' underlined.

"What does that mean to you, Richie?"

Richie looked at it, studied it for a while, then replied, "It means you should attend practice with a positive attitude."

"Well, yes, it does mean that, I suppose," he said, but his tone of voice indicated that wasn't what he would have liked for us to have seen.

"Marc, do you notice anything unusual about the sign?"

I looked the sign over thoroughly, trying to find a hidden message.

"All I can see," I said, "is the word 'make' is underlined and the others aren't."

"That's the key," he said.

"The word 'make' indicates we have a choice of how we will attend a practice session. It suggests we can be either positive or negative, but the choice is ours.

"At Chaucer, we think that is what the 'Yes, But...Theory' does. It lets us choose how we will think.

"When a player dreads going to practice and does nothing about the feeling, he has chosen to attend the session with a negative attitude. Not extremely negative, but to a degree.

"When he neutralizes the feeling with an uplifting statement, he has chosen to be positive.

"Dean, the next time you have a poor attitude toward practice, are you going to choose to be negative or will it be positive?" he asked, kidding him.

"Definitely positive," Dean said forcefully.

The Trojan Horse

Still joking with him, the coach asked him if there was anything else in the gym he would like to make a comment about.

"No! I'm not saying anything else for the rest of the tour!"

We all laughed as we left the gym for the next stop, knowing Dean wasn't going to stay quiet that long.

SUMMARY

- ✔ Like the soldiers in the Trojan Horse, small negatives can enter thoughts unnoticed.
- ✔ They appear small and unimportant, or as something positive.
- ✔ Practice sessions must be approached positively. Improvement takes place there and improvement is largely responsible for success.
- ✔ Guilt feelings must be controlled. Guilt creates negative situations.
- ✔ Regret mistakes, then put them behind you. Don't carry guilt.
- ✔ Forgive yourself. Failure to do so guarantees handicapped performance.
- ✔ Neutralize guilt feelings with a positive statement.
- ✔ The 'Yes, But...Theory' permits us to choose how we will think.

8.
It's How You Take It That Counts

**How our mental picture
is to be painted is our choice.
Winners choose a bright one;
losers pick the dim one.**

As we were about to leave the gym, Coach Norman stopped and began watching the high school girls' basketball team work out.

He showed particular interesting a girl who was shooting lay-ups on a side goal. She would shoot, dribble outside and then drive for another, alternating sides with each shot.

Often, when shooting from the left side, she would dribble out about 40 feet from the goal, then dribble at full speed for a driving shot.

The way she handled the ball and moved about proved she was a good athlete. If she ever missed a shot, I didn't see it.

I turned to the coach and said, "I'll bet the coach is proud of her. She seems very determined and dedicated."

The coach seemed hesitant to agree. He just slowly shook his head up and down, but didn't speak. He continued to watch her.

Finally, he said, "Yes, Marc, the coach is proud of her. She is a good athlete and a very good person, but hold up on your impression of what she is doing. We will talk about her when we get up in the film room."

The basketball coach saw us and came our way.

"Hi, Coach Norman. How's everything today?"

"Fine," he said. "I have four gentlemen here from the University touring our athletic department. I would like you to meet Marc, Dean, Sam and Richie."

Turning to us, he said, "Men, this is Coach Gary Walden, the varsity girls' coach. Coach Walden has also coached boys' basketball and baseball, but feels his personality is best suited for the girls' program, so he has settled in here."

We shook hands and made small-talk about his team and the season, but Coach Norman's attention was still drawn to the girl shooting lay-ups.

SOME PLAYERS COUNT THEIR POSITIVES WHILE OTHERS ADD THEIR NEGATIVES

"Coach Walden, I noticed Joyce is determined to work on her lay-ups." he said without turning his eyes from her.

"Yes," he said rather sadly. "She even came in 15 minutes early to shoot. When I give the team a break, she hurries back to shoot some before we begin another drill.

"Her mental game is presenting a big challenge for me."

Coach Norman looked at the other girls and asked, "Where's Mary? Has she been working on her freethrows?"

"She's over there with the group," Walden said. "No. She has just been doing the normal drills."

"You can't tell any difference in her attitude today?"

Coach Walden shook his head. "No. She's the same Mary as always."

"That's good!"

Coach Norman looked again at the girl shooting the lay-ups. He turned, and with a disappointed look on his face told her coach, "Well, you know how it is, Coach, some count their positives, while others add up their negatives."

I wasn't sure what the meant, but I knew he would explain later.

We walked up a flight of stairs to the video viewing room. Coach Norman suggested we all have a soda while we watch a film.

While he was getting the drinks, he told us the film pertained to the girl who was shooting the lay-ups, and that the film was already in the machine because they had had a counseling session with her just before we arrived this morning.

First, he reviewed us on the mental game, explaining how we feel about

It's How You Take It...

ourselves is very influential in how we perform.

HOW WE 'FEEL' DETERMINES OUR SELF-IMAGE

"There are two important ideas we must remember about the mental picture," he said as he walked to the chalkboard, picked up a piece of chalk, and wrote:

1. The picture is always changing.

2. It is not what happens that changes the picture, but how we feel about the situation.

"I wrote these on the board to help you remember them. It is important you keep these in mind when you're trying to mentally train an athlete.

"How we feel about ourselves, or our mental picture as we call it, is never constant. It's always changing. A basketball player who shoots well in a game may see himself in a positive way, but may adjust the picture if he goes a game without scoring. A baseballer who goes four for five with three runs batted in may have a bright picture, but dim it somewhat after going zero for four with two strikeouts.

"The picture doesn't change just because of the situation, but because of the way we look at the experience.

"For example, the basketball player who failed to score may have a 15-point per game average for the year, and the baseball player who went four at bats without a hit may be a .350 overall hitter. Both averages are good, but they may not be what the players chose to keep in their thoughts.

"The change that happens to their picture will be determined by what they focus on—the average or the poor game.

"This tape," he informed us, "is set at a point where there is only six or seven seconds left in the game."

Turning the tape player on, he hit 'pause' and froze the first image.

WE PAINT WHAT WE FEEL

"This is a film of a recent game between Westwood High and Chaucer. Westwood has the ball and a one-point lead."

He hit the 'play' button to start the action. I recognized number 25 from Chaucer as the girl who had been shooting the lay-ups in practice.

She intercepted a pass and drove the length of the floor for a lay-up. She missed the shot, but one of her teammates got the rebound, went up for a shot, was fouled and missed just as the buzzer sounded ending the game.

She was awarded two freethrows with no time remaining on the clock. She was unable to make either. Chaucer lost the game by one point.

"Let's review this situation," Coach Norman suggested as he turned the power off on the machine. "Joyce missed a lay-up, which would have undoubtedly won the game. Mary missed two freethrows. Making one would have tied the game and given Chaucer a chance to win in overtime, or two makes would have put them ahead one point with no chance for Westwood to score.

"If the situation determined how a player's mental picture is painted, each girl should feel the same. Both had an opportunity to win the game, but neither capitalized on it.

"In this situation the girls didn't react the same. Joyce was extremely dejected and depressed. She felt she had let her team down. She feels she should have worked harder on her lay-ups in the past and now feels she must spend extra hours in the gym practicing them to insure this never happens again.

"Mary, on the other hand, feels she did a good job, but things failed to work out for the best. She feels she did a good job of hustling down the floor to be there for the rebound. She also feels she fought hard for the ball. She thinks she is a good freethrow shooter, but realizes no one can make every shot. She doesn't feel she choked—it just didn't work out the way she wanted it to.

"Here are two identical situations, but the reactions are very different. They are different, not because of the situation, but because of how the two players view the situation.

"Which girl do you think is more apt to have a good performance in the next contest?"

We all agreed we would have more faith in Mary.

"I agree with you," he said, nodding. "I would put my money on Mary because I would be afraid Joyce has smudged her picture of herself. I would be afraid she may not be as confident about her ability as Mary would be.

"Preparing yourself mentally for your next performance is not affected by what happened to you, as much as it is on how you view your experiences."

I asked, "Coach Norman, could you tell us what you told Joyce when you

It's How You Take It... 71

There are people who can look at a situation and see the good. There are others who only see the bad.

counseled her?"

"Sure," he said. "First, let's go back and view the film again."

He ran the tape back to the point just before Joyce intercepted the ball.

DON'T OVERLOOK THE POSITIVES

"It was no accident she intercepted the ball. She had a good defensive position." he explained as he ran the tape forward in slow motion.

"You can see she deflected the ball with the ball-side hand and then outran the opposing player to the ball. When she got the ball, notice that the defense is on the right side of her.

"Joyce is right-handed and was forced to dribble the ball the length of the court with her left hand, which is her weak one. She made a strong dribble all the way with no bobbles. Also, she had good form on the lay-up, but just failed to score.

"The thing we emphasized to Joyce was her choice. She chose to ignore all the good things she did and concentrate on the one negative—the missed shot.

"Also, Joyce failed to remember Chaucer was within one point of Westwood, partly because she had made this type play throughout the game. Without her good play, we would have been farther behind, and would never have had an opportunity to win.

"There are several positives Joyce could have concentrated on, but she didn't choose any of them.

"I told you earlier the mind will only hold one thought at a time, and that one thought will be the most important one.

"Joyce has made the negative the most important and Mary has focused on the positive."

Sam raised his hand slightly. When the coach recognized him, he said, "I've been thinking about what you said earlier. You said the 'Yes, But...Theory' permits the athlete to choose how they will think—positively or negatively. I'm sure you talked to her about the 'Theory', didn't you?"

"We sure did," he replied.

"Then why has she not chosen to think of the positive?"

"That is one of the frustrating parts of mental training," he said.

"Just because you offer someone a ride, doesn't mean they won't choose to go on walking."

It's How You Take It...   73

He paused, giving the question some thought, and then continued, "Have you ever been angry at someone and have another person give you a reason why you shouldn't be so mad? But you are mad, and you don't want to hear a reason why you shouldn't be. You don't want to be happy. You are mad, and you are going to stay that way no matter what anyone says."

Sam laughed. "I guess we have all been guilty of a little bit of that," he said.

"Joyce's feelings may be similar," the coach said. "She probably feels strongly about her feelings of 'letting the team down'.

"Maybe she feels she has a reason to be depressed, and should be dejected. It could be she feels she is guilty, and must bear the guilt.

"You know what I said about guilt. Peak performance and guilty feelings just can't belong to the same person at the same time.

"Joyce is a good player and Coach Walden is good at keeping his players' mental game in order. This problem will be worked out.

"The challenge facing the coach now is to get it worked out as quickly as possible. The longer it takes to clear it up, the longer it will take Joyce to get back to her normal playing form."

Richie asked, "Did you help her form a neutralizing statement to use with the 'Yes, But...Theory'?"

"Yes, we did. We suggested Joyce say, 'Yes, I missed a lay-up which would have won the game, but I had a good game fundamentally and attitude-wise. I didn't give up. I hustled. I didn't loaf, and my play was responsible for Chaucer being within one point at the end'.

"Deep down, Joyce knows she has the opportunity to choose—either to feel good about herself or feel guilty. She is a good player and will eventually choose the positive.

"She knows she did her best, and that will eventually be the most important thought to her. When this happens, the negative will be neutralized and normal play will return."

SUMMARY

- ✔ How we feel about ourselves influences our performance.
- ✔ The mental picture we have of ourselves is never constant. It is always changing.
- ✔ How we accept experiences is more responsible for the picture

changing than is the actual experience itself.
- ✔ The change is due to what we choose as the most important.
- ✔ If the positives are made the most important, our picture will be brighter. Negative thoughts create smudged pictures.
- ✔ The 'Yes, But...Theory' will permit an athlete to choose between positives and negatives only if the desire to think a particular way is present.
- ✔ The 'Theory' doesn't force one to choose, but only permits choice.

9.
'Flash Card' Positives

> **It's better to chase a rabbit and fail than it is to chase a skunk and catch it.**

The 'Yes, But...Theory' seemed so simple, yet questions continued to pop into our minds.

Coach Norman had heard so many 'what if's', 'suppose that's' and 'I don't understand's', it was amazing he continued the tour, but he was still patiently answering every question we asked.

The next 'I don't understand' came from Sam.

REVIEW OF 'THEORY' PRINCIPLES

"Coach Norman, you've sold me on your theory. All the principles make sense to me," he said and then listed them one by one.

"It's less frustrating to admit a problem than it is to deny it.

"The mind can only hold one thought at a time.

"That thought will be the one most important to us.

"A negative will be neutralized when the admission of a mistake is followed by a more important positive.

"And, the 'Theory' will permit one to choose his or her thoughts.

"But, " he said, "one thing frightens me."

"I sure don't want you to leave here afraid of our 'Theory'," Coach said. "What scares you?"

IS THE 'THEORY' TOO TIME CONSUMING?

"Suppose we were playing a basketball game and I made a mistake. To keep from smudging my mental picture, I need to stop, admit the mistake, and then mentally recite a positive statement to counteract it.

"This would take a good deal of time, and I'm afraid the coach would hit me in the back of the head with a basketball if I paused that long while the game was going on."

Sam's description of his coach caused Coach Norman to laugh.

"Sam," he said, "I know your coach and I don't think he would be that brutal, but I get your point.

"It would be disrupting if you were required to go over these statements word for word each time a negative came to your thoughts, but you can put your mind at ease. That's not necessary.

SELF-TALK DIFFERS FROM NORMAL CONVERSATION

"You don't talk to yourself the same way you talk to another person.

"If you were going to tell me your positive statement, you would have to go through it completely so I could understand it, but you don't have to do that when you're talking to yourself.

"The capability of your mind is enormous. It would amaze you how many bits of information your mind is capable of receiving each second.

"Once you've established a positive statement, all that's required is just that you think about it. Every time you think of the statement, you will be flashing a reminder to yourself, and your mind will receive the full meaning.

"It's like a flash card you've seen beforehand, being flashed before your eyes. Since you already know what the card says, you immediately tell yourself what was on it without saying it word for word.

"A sentence is an idea. It's put into words to transfer the idea from one person to another, but you can talk to yourself without using all the words.

"When you see the flash card, you remember what it said and you send the idea immediately to your thoughts without repeating the words.

"Suppose a billboard was on the side of the street you travel every day going to class. The sign is advertising 'XYZ' cars. It says they are smoother,

'Flash Card' Positives

safer and more comfortable.

"One day a friend is riding with you, and just before you pass the sign, he asks, 'What did that sign have on it?'. You only caught a glimpse, but already knew what it said. In an instance, you've told yourself, 'XYZ' cars, smoother, safer, comfortable', but to tell your friend what it said takes considerably more time.

INTERCEPTING THE NEGATIVES

"This rapid self-communication, if used properly, allows us to get a quick start on controlling ill feelings.

"Stopping negatives early, enables us to handle them easier than when we allow them to gain a foothold in our thoughts.

"We've had players who, after becoming experienced using the 'Theory', would reject most adverse effects of negatives just by thinking what they called their 'standard response' to problems.

"For example, the standard response of one particular player was, 'That's not the most important thing'.

"He responded with this one standard response to everything that happened to him that had a negative tint.

"He didn't say all six words to himself. He just communicated the idea to his mind. To say all the words takes at least two seconds. To think the idea takes less than half of a second with the same effect. The mind will get the full message.

"Just by thinking this thought, the athlete flashed several possible, positive thoughts to himself without saying them.

"Since he had had experience formulating positive statements using the 'Yes, But...Theory', it wasn't necessary to go through the entire process of admitting the problem existed, and following it with a more important positive statement.

"The standard response was 'flash carding' positives to his thoughts.

"If he made an infield error in baseball and thought, 'That's not the most important thing', he was flashing to his mind, 'Yes, I made an error, but everyone makes mistakes', or 'Yes, I made an error, but that's not my normal self; I'm better than that'.

"If a pitcher fooled him on a curve ball, instead of saying, 'Yes, the pitcher fooled me on that pitch, but I'm a good curve ball hitter and will probably hit the next one he throws', he flashed the entire idea to himself just by thinking his standard response.

"He had had enough experience with the 'Theory' he was able to condense it to one standard statement and still transmit numerous positives to his mind.

"He was intercepting the negatives before they entrenched themselves in his thoughts. This was simpler than trying to neutralize ingrained, bad thoughts.

"Thinking one standard thought is like a trigger shooting out interceptors to turn back negatives.

"So, you see, Sam." Coach Norman said, "there's no need to fret about irritating the coach by having to stop your play to fight negatives.

"The more you use the 'Theory', the more condensed and refined you will get it until it's almost automatic, and very little time will be needed."

"Would you suggest a beginner create a 'standard response'?" Sam asked.

"No, I don't believe I would recommend a player just learning the 'Theory' use a standard thought.

"It wouldn't be harmful, but I would be afraid he would try to depend on it without developing good, positive, counteracting statements.

"I would recommend all players, both experienced and beginners, mentally repeat the entire 'Yes, But...Theory' word for word when the situation permits. Recite the admission of the problem and all words in the counteracting statement.

"This will help train oneself to use the 'Theory'. It will insure good, positive thoughts are being created, and each positive, counteracting statement formulated will be filed away in the mind, ready to be flashed before the mind's eye when only a standard response can be used.

"The more of these statements you have formulated, the better chance you'll have of a standard response being effective during a game.

"In short, it's not necessary to recite the entire statement of the 'Theory', but when time allows, go ahead and do it anyway."

SUMMARY

✔ We can communicate with ourselves at almost lightning speed.

✔ We do not have to recite a sentence word for word when talking to

'Flash Card' Positives

ourselves. We 'talk' in ideas rather than words.
- ✔ A standard response can be substituted for the 'Theory' statement after gaining some experience.
- ✔ The more the 'Theory' is used, the more condensed and refined it will become.
- ✔ If time permits, counteracting statements should be formulated and used. This will build a mental file of positives to be flashed to the mind later.

10.
Habits

> **Breaking habits can be compared
> to coming down a set of stairs.
> You don't jump from the top step
> to the bottom landing.
> You come down one step at a time.**

"The approach to mental training will become more condensed and refined with experience. Is that right?" Richie questioned the coach.

"Yes," Coach Norman confirmed. "Everytime you use the program, you gain experience and become more understanding of how it works. You automatically smooth out the way you apply it to your situations."

EFFICIENCY AND EASE INCREASES WITH USE

"Well, does being condensed and refined mean it will be more efficient and easier?" Richie continued his questioning.

"Yes. Most definitely yes!" the coach said emphatically.

"Mental training is no different than practicing fundamentals.

"The more you practice a fundamental, the more apt you are to perfect it. The same holds true for your mental training. The more you practice it, the more efficient it will be.

"Every time you attempt to be positive, you are practicing your mental game.

"After using the 'Theory' a while, we began to counteract negatives automatically."

"That sounds like it would be a good situation to be in," Richie said, "but how would we ever reach a condition like that?"

"It's not as difficult as it may sound," the coach said.

"We are, by nature, creatures of habit. What we do one time, we have a tendency to do again and again.

"Being habitual makes life easier. It requires less thought and effort to do things which come automatic than it does to do something a different way.

"How we think and act are no exceptions to this natural tendency to do something over and over the same way. People who are happy have developed a habit of being joyous. The same thing goes for those who are grumpy.

"A person who has a positive attitude will consistently see the good in anything. A negative thinking person will hardly ever see the positive.

"They have made it a habit to think a particular way."

Puzzled, Richie asked, "Are you suggesting a player who plays with fear and one who plays courageously does so because of habit?"

"There may be exceptions, but generally speaking, that's true," the coach replied.

"It's not that they have developed a habit of being afraid, but fear develops when anyone continually sees and emphasizes those things which cause doubt.

"Doubt causes fear.

"They lack courage during a performance because they have developed a habit of doubting.

"A few years ago we had an extremely talented quarterback. As a junior, his confidence would come and go like the daily sunset. He was forever finding situations in his performance that would cause him to doubt himself.

"The coaches worked very closely with him. Every time something happened causing him to question his ability, they would help him develop a positive statement to neutralize the problem. He would say, 'Yes' (and admit the problem), and say 'but'(and insert a more important positive).

"The player dedicated himself to avoiding all negative self-talk, and by the time he was a senior he had developed a habit of being confident.

"You see, Richie, if we can get players rejecting those thoughts that cause doubt, by either intercepting them before they enter their mind, or neutralizing them once they have gained a foothold in their thoughts, they will be concentrating on those things that lead to courage. This, in turn, will lead to courageous play.

"Once it becomes habitual, thinking positively will be the easiest because is will be automatic. Thinking negatively will require more effort because it isn't a habit.

"What we do habitually, we do the easiest.

"If we can get the athletes to a point where they begin to make positive thinking a habit, we will be heading toward the ideal situation.

OUR INNER ALARM SYSTEM

"When a player consistently challenges negative thoughts, he begins to develop an inner alarm system.

"He will remind himself each time a negative thought begins to surface in his mind.

"It's almost as if a little bell rings every time a negative thought threatens.

"He doesn't have to rid his mind of these negatives because he intercepts and turns them away before they enter.

"When this point is reached, fears, doubts, anxieties and apprehensions will find it difficult to penetrate the thinking.

"When this happens both the athletic performance and life in general will be more satisfying and contented."

SUMMARY

- ✔ Each time the 'Theory' is used, it becomes easier to do.
- ✔ The mental game should be practiced just as fundamentals are practiced.
- ✔ The more the mental game is practiced, the better it will be.
- ✔ The mental game is practiced each time positive thinking is atttempted.

- ✔ We are all creatures of habit.
- ✔ Thinking positively or negatively can be habitual.
- ✔ Habits are easier to perform than non-habits, because it takes less effort and thought to do something we are in a habit of doing.

11.
Don't Reverse
The Theory

**No athlete is so good he can't
give a compliment.
No athlete is so bad he can't
be given a compliment.**

In a recent psychology class we had studied a philosophy that seemed to disagree with Coach Norman's theory.

This idea suggested avoiding using 'but' when trying to improve self-esteem and confidence. But, here, he was telling us to use the word to help develop good feelings.

I outlined the belief to the coach, and asked him to explain how using 'but' in one case would be good and in another, harmful.

"I agree with those authors completely," he said, confusing us.

"We have discussed the 'Theory' enough you should have an understanding of the importance of using 'but'.

"Tell me what 'but' does to a statement," he said to me.

"It lessens the importance of the preceding statement," I said. "or you could say it degrades the statement it follows."

"I like the use of 'degrading'," he said.

"That's what we're trying to do. DEGRADE THE NEGATIVES AND UPGRADE THE POSITIVES.

"What these authors are saying is, 'don't use but to degrade the positive'.

"This can happen. All you have to do is reverse the process we've been talking about."

THE POWER OF THE WORD "BUT"

You had a poor start.

Yes, BUT I was still able to win the race.

It can help change a negative into a positive or........

You sure ran a good race.

Yes, BUT I had a poor start.

help change a positive into a negative.

Don't Reverse The Theory

"Could you give me an example of how to do this?" I asked.

"Sure. That's easy." he said. "Suppose you are the quarterback of your football team. One of the ends makes a cut across the field. He is well defended and it would take a perfect pass for him to be able to catch it. Your pass is exactly where it should be, he catches it, and runs for a touchdown.

"Later, in the dressing room, a reporter congratulates you on the perfect pass, and you reply something like: 'Yes, It was a good pass, but I will probably never be able to make another like it'.

"By saying this, what would you have done?" he asked.

"I would have degraded the fact I made a good pass."

"Yes," he said. "You have admitted you made a good pass, degraded it with 'but', and added a more important negative statement.

"Remember, the mind can only hold one thought at a time, and that one thought will be the one most important to you.

"To an athlete with any degree of pride, believing he will never throw another perfect pass will be more influential to his career than the fact he did throw one. Therefore, his thoughts will be on maybe never again throwing a good pass.

"That's not a very good thought for an athlete to carry into a performance, is it?

"You've taken something that could boost your self-esteem, and degraded it to the point it may harm future performances.

"Our 'Theory' and the philosophy you mentioned, are in complete agreement. We are saying, use 'but' to degrade the negative, and they are saying, don't use 'but' to degrade the positive.

"Our idea will do the same thing you studied unless you put ours in reverse order.

"Do you understand how they agree?"

"Yes," I said. "But can degrade any statement it follows. Just be sure the one preceding it is a negative. If it should be a positive, your mental game will suffer."

NEVER USE 'BUT' TO DEGRADE A COMPLIMENT

"Another thing following this same idea, is how we receive a compliment," Coach Norman said.

"Compliments should lift us up. They should be encouraging to our self-esteem, but many negative-thinking people prevent this build up.

"Many players have difficulty accepting compliments. They feel they must qualify them. For example, when a player is congratulated on a good game, he may say, 'Thanks, but I was just lucky', or 'I really don't think I did too well'.

"Instead of just saying 'thanks' and going on, they degrade it until it becomes a negative.

"I told you earlier, 'but' can be a very influential word. Be careful how you use it. It can be beneficial. It can be harmful.

"Don't put our 'Theory' in reverse. If you do, you may degrade the good."

SUMMARY

- ✔ When the 'Yes, But...Theory' is used correctly, it can be beneficial.
- ✔ When it's put in reverse order, it can be harmful.
- ✔ Accept compliments with a simple 'thanks'. Don't degrade it or feel it must be qualified.

12.
Tour Wrap Up

**We have a choice of how we feel.
We can doubt or build
confidence. It's our choice.**

As we walked back toward the AD's office to prepare to return to the University, Coach Norman wrapped up all he had taught us during the tour with this talk:

BE A STUDENT OF YOUR SPORT

I told you at the beginning of your visit here, to always be a student and a teacher of your sport. Learn all you can from others, and be just as quick to teach them.

Don't let your ego get in the way of becoming more proficient.

Never be afraid to ask questions, and always give an honest answer when asked.

No one knows everything. We all have room to improve. Take advantage of any advice or help you can get.

WHAT MAKES CONSISTENT WINNERS?

Each of you had the same question when you arrived this morning—why do some teams and individuals win consistently while others face day-to-day struggles?

Consistent winning doesn't come from only physical skill and knowledge of the game. Teams and participants must also be prepared mentally.

Championships can't be reached before we 'feel' we are champions. As long as doubts and fears are present, we can't develop confidence. Without confidence, championship performance is impossible.

To feel like champions, doubt and fear must be kept at a minimum. For years, people in the sports world have believed we can do nothing about this. They felt players were just naturally fearful or courageous; that they were born that way and nothing could be done to correct it.

I hope you see we do have a choice of how we feel.

We can create doubt, or we can build confidence. It's our choice.

Doubt overcomes us not just because of our inadequacies, but because we 'feel' inadequate. We have trained ourselves to be doubting. We have done this by habitually concentrating on those characteristics that suggest we're not capable.

We've made it a habit to think, I'm too short; too slow; too big; not big enough; or the coach doesn't like me. All these cause us to doubt our potential. But, remember, there is always a positive that can be substituted for these thoughts.

Find them. Use them. Make it a habit of rejecting those defeating thoughts. Get in the habit of thinking good things about yourself.

You'll be amazed at how many good traits you can find about youself. The more you search for them, the more positive you'll be. Your confidence will escalate because you're finding more and more proof you are capable.

THE YES, BUT THEORY

This theory has the potential to help you become a confident and successful player, but there is one warning.

It would be a mistake to consider the 'Theory' an immediate, painless remedy to solve all problems. Nothing has ever been discovered that will do that, and most likely, never will.

The 'Theory' is only a helper. It will help young athletes develop necessary characteristics to be successful in sports.

The 'Yes, But...Theory' is a simple and effective tool to help you become the best you can be. But it needs one thing. It needs you. It needs your dedication, determination and desire. Without you, it's useless; with you and these traits, the potential is almost unlimited.

One of the greatest strengths of this 'Theory' is its simplicity.

It's not necessary to remember a lot of information or procedures. All that's needed is to admit your problem, and neutralize it with something good that's more important to you than the negative. Your mind will choose to think about the most important, and the negative's importance will be degraded.

Also, the one 'Yes, But...' statement will work on most situations.

The one statement can be used to develop confidence, satisfaction, morality, team play, and hundreds of other positive traits.

ROAD TO SUCCESS

The 'Theory' isn't magic. It would be a mistake to include this, or any mental training program, expecting it to wash away all problems immediately.

Effective, yes, but "Yes, But..." are not some hocus-pocus words that can be said and 'poof', a fairy godmother appears with a magic wand to vanish problems forever from your life.

Everyone has problems. This 'Theory' is an instrument to help you fight through them so you can continue.

There is no four-lane highway to success for anyone.

Many times it's assumed successful people were born with great talent and just 'breezed' to the top.

Few successful performers have made it to the top without having to fight to get there.

One thing is certain: no successful person has made it with negative thoughts dominating his mind. The 'Theory' allows you to cut yourself loose from those negatives, rather than drag them throughout your career.

Those people who have made their lives a success may not have used the 'Yes, But...Theory', but they lived by the same principle. They filled their minds with good feelings about themselves. Feelings that encouraged them to push forward and upward.

Consciously or unconsciously, they found the good in the situations that confronted them. They let these occupy their thoughts.

If it were possible for us to go back down the road some successful person traveled, we would be amazed that he or she faced the same things faced by those who gave up.

We would find many places where tears had been shed, and where frustration surrounded them completely. Also, we would see where they had failed and slid back down in their climb to stardom.

We would see the same things that are on roads traveled by many who gave up and quit. In many cases the difference would be the fight the winner had within himself. The winner failed to give in to the setbacks.

When the road gets rocky and rough, stop and look, there will be two sets of footprints. One set was made by those who gave up and went back down the hill. The other set was made by those who wouldn't give up. They fought their way through the obstacle and continued on up the mountain of success.

The 'Theory' will let you say, 'Yes, it is going to be tough and demanding, but I can see where I want to go and will continue until I get there'. It will help you crawl over many of the detours obstructing the paths of any athletic hopeful.

THE TOUGHEST OPPONENT

Your toughest opponent doesn't live in another school district. He lives within your own body.

You are your toughest opponent. Much of your success depends on how serious you are about competing with yourself.

Your challenge is to be better today than 'you yesterday', and 'you tomorrow' to be better than 'you today'.

To be better than 'you in the past' is improvement, and improvement is your ride to success.

To reach success you must have a ticket on the 'improvement express'. It's the only transportation that goes there.

Daily improvement is the key to success.

To consistently improve, we must face and win the daily battles to out-do 'yesterday's self'.

Improvement is shortening the distance between potential and actual performance.

FUNDAMENTAL PRACTICE

Mental training is important to any program, but it doesn't take away the need to practice fundamentals.

An athlete's success depends on improvement; continual, everyday improvement.

Negatives and problems cause countless hours of practice, with no improvement. Since practice time is limited, the less time wasted, the more we can accomplish. The 'Theory' makes it possible to degrade or eliminate problems, creating an atmosphere that encourages progress.

Good luck on your road to athletic success. May you always travel over rough places in the arms of the positive rather than be pulled back by the grappling fingers of negatives."

13.
Good bye Chaucer High

**Team members shouldn't be like
a hitch hiker, who lets others
pay the expenses and rides free.
There's a price to pay
for success. Contribute your share.**

I had mixed feelings as we walked toward our car to return to the University.

I felt anxious. I wanted to get back and begin adapting these ideas to my own career, but I also wished I could spend more time acquainting myself with Chaucer's mental training.

Coach Norman walked with us continuing to talk about the 'Theory'.

THE HITCH HIKER

As we crossed the campus, a young man came around the corner of a building, hurrying toward the football practice field.

The coach shook his head and chuckled. When he came within hearing distance the coach said, "Hello, Mike. Late again?"

"Oh, maybe a minute or two, Coach," he replied and continued his quick pace toward the field.

"Mike is what we call a 'hitch hiker' athlete," he said.

"A hitch hiker?" Dean asked. "Doesn't he have a car?"

"He has a car. His problem is, he treats athletics the same way a hitch hiker does traveling.

"A hitch hiker stands on the side of the road with his thumb out. He lets others buy the car, furnish the gasoline, pay for the upkeep and insurance on the automobile, and he goes along for a free ride.

"Many athletes are the same. They want to ride without paying the price.

"Chances of success are improved when players do what needs to be done, not just what they are required to do. On a team, every job is everyone's responsibility, whether it's helping get ready for practices, assisting with the laundry, boosting someone's morale, or offering encouragement."

"Will the 'Yes, But...Theory' help this type player?" Dean asked.

"I don't know of anything positive thoughts wouldn't help," the coach said, "but the problem is getting the player wanting to improve. "Until a player wants to change, nothing will work.

THE PLAYER IS THE PILOT

"To stop the influence of a negative, a positive must be substituted, and only the person holding the thought can do that.

"Disturbed players often turn to their coaches for answers. Coaches can offer advice, but until the player accepts the suggestions and inserts them into his thoughts, they will do no good.

"It's like a pilot who loses control of his aircraft, and it goes into a dive. Someone on the ground may offer advice by radio, but until the pilot puts the advice into action, the plane will continue its descent.

"It makes no difference how much advice is given, unless the pilot pulls back on the controls, the plane will plunge into the ground."

WILDFIRE

Sam said, "I remember us having a hitch hiker player. His actions were always causing dissension on our team. It seemed he was always causing someone to become angry."

"They can do that," Coach Norman agreed, "and arguing, criticizing and teammates degrading each other are sure signs of trouble ahead for any athletic team.

"These things destroy peace and harmony and jeopardize success.

"Dissension is like wildfire. Unless it's put out quickly, it can ruin everything.

"Future successes are like the prairie in front of the fire—in danger of being destroyed."

THE THREE OF 'ME'

"Coach Norman," I asked, "what do you think is the most important thing the 'Theory' can do for an athlete?"

"There's no doubt," he said, "that the most important thing it can do is help the player play as close to his potential as possible.

"It has been said athletes are really three different players. The player they THINK they are, the player OTHERS THINK they are, and the player they ACTUALLY ARE. What others think we are has no influence on performance. We're concerned about the difference between what we think we can do, and what we're capable of doing.

"The person you think you are will probably be the person that shows up for the ball game, because you usually play close to the way you think you can.

"What we should do is attempt to get the person that we think we are to equal the person we really are.

"There is usually a large difference between the two. Therefore, there's a big difference between our current performance and our possible performance.

"It would be unrealistic to believe we could ever reach 100 percent of our potential, but it's a shame for us not to try to get as close as possible."

NARROWING THE GAP

"Coach," I said, "could you give me an example of how we could narrow the distance between what we are doing and what we could do?"

"Sure. Do you have a situation in mind?"

"Well, suppose we had a hitch hiker type player. How would the 'Theory' maneuver him into becoming a better player?"

The coach thought for a little while, and said, "Let's assume this make-believe player wants to change. He lists his negative qualities on a piece of paper, and one of them is 'I'm fairly lazy'.

"The image of being a lazy player would be negative and harmful to his performance because no one can play his best, feeling he's lazy.

"If he used the 'Yes, But...Theory' and said, 'Yes, I'm a fairly lazy person, but I'm going to improve. I'm going to work on being more energetic and dedicated'. Would this change his self-image? Yes it would.

"He would probably still see himself as being slightly lazy, but his predominate thought would be one of improving. He's going to be better. He's on the mend.

"It's almost as if being lazy is in the past. He now sees himself as an improving player, and images of improvement are much more positive than laziness.

"With this new view of himself, there's a good chance he'll perform better because he feels better about himself.

"He hasn't just altered the mental picture. He has changed the physical person.

"He has shortened the gap between what's possible and what's real.

CHANGE CAN BE GOOD OR BAD

"This player has 'redecided' what kind of player he is. He wasn't chained to the type player he imagined himself to be.

"Be aware that when he changed his view of himself in relationship to being lazy, that didn't make it permanent.

"He still has the choice of 'redeciding'. It would be easy for him to redecide that he is a 'fairly lazy person'.

"He will revert back to the person he was before the redecision unless he carries through with the idea of improving his laziness. Redecision can be for the better, or for the worse."

ATTITUDE TOWARD LOSSES

We reached the parking lot and went to our car, but none of us made a move to get in. It seemed Coach Norman was also finding it hard to find a quitting place. He continued his discussion of the mental game.

It was Richie who was the next to keep the discussion going. "Coach, I have a friend I think could benefit from this philosophy. If I give you the problem, will you tell me what you would do? If you will, maybe I can help him."

It didn't surprise us when he said he would.

"This friend is on the track team. In a recent meet he was running the anchor leg of the 440-yard relay. He was given the baton with a slight lead, but lost the lead before reaching the finish line. Losing that event caused our team to come in second. He feels completely responsible for the team failing to win, and it has caused him to go through a great deal of guilt and turmoil. The rest of the team don't blame him, but he blames himself."

"I've seen situations like this many times," the coach said.

"I told you earlier, it's not the experience, but how one reacts to the experience that influences our image.

"If you are a tennis player, wrestler, golfer, or trackster that has lost a crucial match, how are you going to react to it? Are you going to suggest to yourself that you are a poor performer, and that you let your teammates and school down? Are you going to feel everyone in town, from the mayor to the school crossing guard, looks at you as a community disgrace?

"You can have a real 'pity party', and send a basket full of 'oh, no's' to your innerself, and really smudge your self-image, or you can understand that in sports, as in everyday life, nothing goes perfectly all of the time.

"You can remind yourself that improvement usually comes from defeat more than it does from winning, and let the positives be the basis for your predominate thoughts.

"Much of your future success depends on what you choose as your major thoughts. You had better choose the positives.

"Use the 'Yes, But...Theory' or something similiar, or the next performance may be in trouble.

"Should you try to block out the match? Should you try to forget that it ever happened? No! It doesn't matter how hard you try, you will never forget that you lost the crucial event. No matter how hard you try, you will always wish you had won. The important thing is to make sure it doesn't cause your next performance to be a poor one.

"Admit that, 'yes, I performed; yes, it was crucial; and yes, I lost. Yes, this all happened, but it will make me a better performer. I know what I did wrong and I will work to perfect it before the next match.

"'Yes, I'm dejected right now, but with the determination caused by the loss there will be more success to enjoy in the future.

"'Yes, to some, this may be classified as a failure, but to me it's a stepping stone to improvement'.

"The positive ideas, not the negatives, must be the most dominating."

"Thanks," Richie said. "Those negative feelings you described come pretty close to the way he is reacting. Maybe I can help him work through this problem."

"Your friend needs to realize that the thoughts that go through our mind are probably the greatest influence on the way we perform.

"Good feelings such as confidence, courage, and hope have a tendency to cause us to play better, while fear, and lack of confidence and hope tends to destroy good play.

"We can't play with confidence as long as we doubt our capabilities. It's impossible to play courageously as long as we are overcome by fear, nor can we play relaxed and poised when our muscles are restricted by tension.

"All of our feelings, both good and bad, are created by the thoughts we choose to think."

WE HAVE BOTH GOOD AND BAD FEELINGS ABOUT OURSELVES

"Do we have both good and bad feelings about ourselves?" Dean asked.

"Yes." he said. "A good example of having both, is a baseball player who has great confidence against right handed pitchers, but feels he just can't get a hit off lefties.

"This is two different types of players going to the plate. When a right handed pitcher is on the mound, the batter is confident, relaxed, and expecting to hit the ball.

"When a left hander is throwing, a completely different player goes to the plate. This player has no composure or poise. His swing is restricted by his tense muscles. He doesn't think about where he wants to hit the ball, he just wants to get his bat on it without striking out.

"Here is the same player with the same athletic ability, but in no way does his potential compare.

"In this particular case, a small percentage of the fault is physical, but the rest is mental.

"He has created good feelings by telling himself he is good at hitting righthanders, but has created bad feelings by concentrating on his problem of hitting left handers.

"All of us are like the baseball player. We've developed both good and bad feelings about our capabilities.

"To be the best we can be, we must help those good feelings grow, and eliminate the bad.

"Feelings of confidence leads to smooth and relaxed performance while fear restricts.

"Once we learn to choose our thoughts, improvement should follow."

SMILE—A GOOD WEAPON AGAINST TENSION

A bell rang signaling the end of the school day at Chaucer High School. Students and faculty members came to the parking lot, got in their cars and drove away. Only one car remained, and we could see a faculty member coming toward it.

"Here comes Coach Hardy, the tennis coach," Coach Norman said. "He has a story I would like for him to tell you.

"Coach Hardy, this is Dean, Sam, Richie and Marc. They've been visiting our school today discussing mental training."

After we all shook hands, he asked the tennis coach, "Would you relate the story of Rob Brown and his tennis serve?"

"Certainly," he said. "A couple of years ago we had a tennis player named Rob Brown. He was one of our most dependable players.

"One of Rob's strengths was his serve. Even the better players had trouble returning it.

"He began to lose his confidence. He lost two out of three matches and his play was progressively getting worse. Players who had normally felt satisfied just to get the ball back over the net were now making strong returns. An advantage Rob once had was gone.

"Coach Norman and I talked to him and it was evident only negative thoughts were going through his mind. He talked of 'hitting the net'; 'double faults'; 'the serve was easy for the opponent to handle'; and 'what had been an advantage for him was now a disadvantage'.

"He confirmed our belief that he no longer trusted his serve. He admitted that earlier he was not afraid of just barely clearing the net on the serve, but now he felt he was forced to keep the ball higher. Also, where he had once tried to hit close to the out-of-bound lines, he now would aim more to the middle. He had even eased up on his serve to improve accuracy.

"This player who had been one of the state's best was quickly becoming an average performer."

I had been through slumps in baseball, and could sympathize with him.

"That must have been a miserable time for him," I said.

"It sure was," he agreed.

"Did you use the 'Yes, But...Theory' with him?"

"We did, but he was unable to use it effectively. He just couldn't feel there was a positive more important than his poor serve.

"Coach Norman finally came up with a new 'twist' that got Rob on the road to recovering his form.

"Coach," he said to Coach Norman, "tell them what you did."

"Okay," he said. "First, I had him do what we have all young players do; admit the problem. I had him say, 'Yes, I am having trouble with my serve'.

"As he said it, he was grim and tense. That is what negative thinking does. It creates tension.

"There was too much emotion in the way he said it, and I wouldn't accept it.

"I had him take a couple of deep breaths and relax as much as possible. I even suggested that if he had a girlfriend, to think of her and at the same time casually say, 'Yes, I'm having trouble with my serve'.

"This helped some, but there was still tension. So, we did it again.

"The next time, I had him smile as he said it. I didn't want a nervous smile, but a truly happy smile.

"He did, and I could see we were making progress. It was better because he admitted the problem without making it sound as if it was a 'life or death' situation.

"Many players have been calmed with a smile from a coach or parent, or smiling themselves.

"Have you ever tried to put a smile on your face and tense your muscles at the same time? It's hard to do. How many times have you seen anyone involved in a serious argument with a happy smile on his face?

"Many times smiles will do wonders with tenseness and nervousness.

"When Rob smiled as he admitted the problem, he had reduced much of the importance, but it was still his main thought.

"We still had to counteract the negative, but the smile put the problem in a perspective that permitted a neutralizing statement to work.

"Rob worked through his slump, had a successsful season, and is now playing tennis in college."

THE GREAT WASTE

Coach Hardy looked at his watch and said, "Coach, you haven't forgotten we have a departmental meeting this afternoon, have you?"

"Oh, that's right," he said. "Well, gentlemen, I guess the clock is going to force us to stop our discussion whether we want to or not."

"I certainly appreciate each of you visiting our school, and I've enjoyed our discussion.

"Before I go, there's one other point I would like to make.

"There's a terrible waste going on in the world. It's greater than the waste of soil, water and oil. The waste is the individual's ability to succeed.

"Men and women with the ability to become doctors, lawyers or business executives are living lives of mediocrity. Those who could be professional athletes are setting in the stands eating hotdogs while others play the game. Thousands of young people each year who have the ability to live a long and happy life are committing suicide. Every area of the United States has a large group of people wasting the one life they have on drugs, alcohol, or just moving from place to place searching for something to give their life some meaning.

"When a person's success falls far below his capabilities, that's a waste!

"You young men will have the opportunity to help youngsters avoid this loss. I encourage you to do your best for them.

"I must go, gentlemen. Goodbye."

None of us spoke. We just got into the car and sat in silence watching Coach Norman walk across the campus and go into the gym.

Finally, I started the car and pulled onto Highway 22 headed toward the University.

No one said a word. It was as if we were in a trance thinking of all we had seen and heard.

Richie brought us out of it when he calmly said, "I've seen tons."

"You've seen tons of what?" Sam said with a giggle.

"I've seen tons of one of the greatest commodites on earth wasted, and didn't even know it was happening. In fact, I've been one of those wasting the ability to succeed, but my goal will be to do all I can to avoid this in my life, and the lives of others.

We all nodded and returned to our silence.

PART TWO

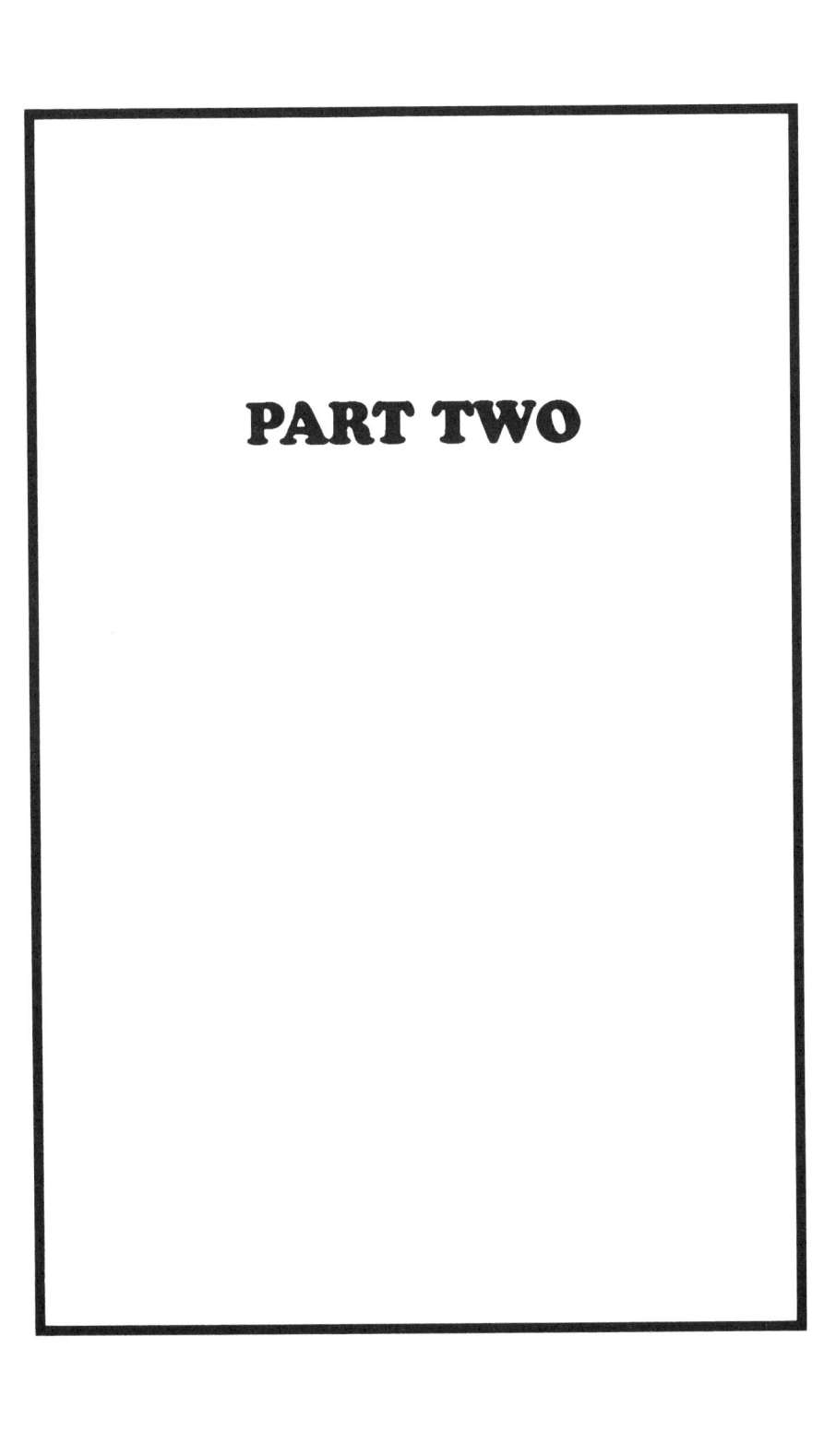

Guidance Tips For Coaches and Parents

This section was designed specifically to help parents and coaches lead their youngsters to a more improved performance, but athletes, too, are encouraged to study it. It will help them strengthen their mental approach to athletics.

This portion of the book is designed to be studied in coordination with Part One, "Plan To Win". To get the best understanding, it is recommended Part One be read first.

INTRODUCTION

During the past two decades, the study of athletic behavior has been presented to the sports world in book after book, based on highly scientific research and studies.

The validity of these studies is, in no way, questioned, but the usefulness of some of them to the young athlete, and average coach or parent can be.

These studies have became so involved, many people become lost long before they reach any degree of comprehension.

The purpose of this program isn't to attempt to 'break out on top' with some great new revelation. It is, rather, to go back in time before the term 'sports psychology' was coined, pick up the pieces of what was known then, and attempt to put them in terms our young people can understand and use today.

The intention isn't to create olympic gold medalists nor to help a silver medal winner take another step up the ceremonial podium. It's directed to those young people who play only a few, short years, purely for enjoyment.

This book and its program isn't aimed at an audience of big university or professional coaches and players because, although some could benefit from it, most are already passed this level.

It is aimed at thoses coaches who are dedicated to making local sports enjoyable.

I want to inform parents on the mental aspects of sports, hoping in some way, it will make their years in the stands watching their child, as well as the player's few years on the court or field as enjoyable and satisfying as possible.

14. Total Athletic Training

> **Performance equals self-evaluation. Seldom does a player play better than his expectations.**

The topic at a recent coaches' gathering turned to "why some teams win year after year while others never seem to be contenders for any championships."

One coach pointed out that almost every coach uses the same type of drills to train their teams and, also, variations of the same offensive and defensive sets. Yet, the winners continue to win while the others remain mediocre.

Usually, natural athletic ability is credited. People complain that it isn't fair that another school continues to have great athletes year after year while they must attempt to contend with less talented players.

Granted, there are times when one school does have a run of good athletes while another must participate with less-talented players. It happens, but it isn't the main reason for consistent success or mediocrity.

There's another reason.

Usually winning and losing isn't determined by how much ability one has, but how effectively the talent is used.

THE MENTAL GAME

All athletes have physical traits like running, jumping, throwing and lifting. These are important to success, but another group of characteristics is just as important to success as the physical. Every player has these.

This group of traits, commonly called the mental game of the athlete, includes confidence, playing under pressure, teamwork, not allowing a miscue or failure to disrupt them, accepting responsibility for both failure and success, always being positive, and striving for perfection but accepting the outcome whatever it may be.

A player can't be consistently successful without first mastering these traits.

A basketball player who has lost his confidence can't be successful no matter how high he can jump or how fast he can run.

A golfer with great potential can't play effectively if he can't reach that degree of relaxation necessary for a good swing.

A baseball pitcher, regardless of talent, will never be able to consistently throw strikes that will get a good hitter out if he has doubts and negative thoughts racing through his mind.

The effectiveness of talent is lessened when the mental frame of mind is negative.

Good performance depends on things like mental toughness, concentration and composure.

Coaches are referring to these aspects of the game when they say a team 'has lost it's cool', 'had a mental lapse' or 'momentum changed'.

It has been estimated as much as 75 to 90 percent of good performance depends on the mental game. The importance has been recognized, but most admit that less than 10 percent of practice time is devoted to mental training.

The amount of improvement one can expect in running, jumping and throwing is limited, but the potential for improving most young athlete's mental game is enormous.

A baseball player who can get from homeplate to first base in 4 seconds flat after hitting a ball, can expect little improvement no matter how much he works on it. But there is a great deal of potential for improving the batting average of a hitter who has a 'mental block' when going against fast ball pitchers.

Research and tests are producing more and more evidence that support the idea that after learning the fundamentals of the game, more progress can be made by improving one's frame of mind than by drilling only the physical.

Most coaches, until recently, considered the mental traits to be natural and not trainable.

They were wrong! We weren't born confident or able to play under pressure. Experiences and situations throughout life have caused us to develop these positive traits.

Today, there is little doubt that athletic training must be approached with the mental in mind as well as the physical.

Mental traits are trainable and can be refined. Negative mental traits are not something we were born with, must live with and die with. Unfortunately, all too often, that's the case, but it doesn't have to be.

SELF-EVALUATION

There is no guarantee an athlete with lots of athletic ability will perform well. This is one of the greatest frustrations facing coaches, parents and players at all levels—why two players with equal ability don't always perform equally, and why players with limited ability often outperform others with much more talent.

The reason Johnny or Mary don't perform up to their potential is often caused by the player's own self-evaluation.

All players have rated themselves as a particular type player with a certain amount of ability.

Players have 'decided' what their potential is. Based on past experiences and situations, they have decided they are average, below average or above average.

This has a tremendous effect on the way they play, because performance usually equals self-evaluation. Very seldom will a player play better than his or her expectations.

Players restrict themselves to this 'decided' level by their frame of mind, not athletic ability.

Players with great ability, but who fail to perform well, may have mastered the physical, but not the mental. Those who excel with limited ability, have mastered the mental enough to overcome the handicap of not being overly talented.

The good news is, players are not permanently caged in their 'decided' level. Everyone has the ability to 'redecide'. All have the power to re-evaluate themselves.

The bad news is, most coaches, parents and players fail to pursue the redeciding route, but continue to stress the physical to overcome a problem caused by the mental.

DON'T FEED THE WRONG NEED

A poise or confidence problem won't be cured by practicing physical fundamentals.

It's like an automobile engine. It needs both oil and gasoline to operate efficiently. Gasoline gives it the power to turn the crankshaft, and oil eliminates friction. If the engine runs out of oil, friction restricts movement. It doesn't matter how much more gasoline is added to the fuel tank, the friction caused by the lack of oil remains.

Just as an automobile needs oil to run smoothly, the athlete with sufficient fundamental skills, but insufficient mental skills, needs mental training to perform well.

MENTAL TRAINING MATERIAL

Availability of information regarding mental training, or sports psychology, as it is called, is no problem.

After the East Germans and Russians began to emphasize mental training in the 1960's and 70's, there has been an explosion in the study of the mind's influence on performance.

Almost overnight, coaches and athletes all over the world wanted to know how to stop the mind from interfering with good performance. Almost all universities now have classes related to performance. Many are offering graduate degrees in the field.

A relatively large library could be filled with books outlining methods to improve the mental game.

Considering all the information available today about mental training, it's unfair that any young athlete should be denied the opportunity to fully develop his or her potential in sports.

WHY IS THE MENTAL GAME IGNORED?

The reason mental training is limited is not lack of dedication or concern. Any athlete with pride wants to improve, and there are few coaches who aren't willing to do all they can to make their team one of the best.

The problem is the application of available knowledge.

How is this information from volumns of studies to be applied to a junior high or high school athletic program?

Young coaches study mental training books, but have no plan of presentation. They struggle with it awhile and become even more confused. It's frustrating to the parents of a ten-year-old when they can't find a way to impart to their child the information they possess.

What happens? They toss it aside and attempt to overcome any mental deficiencies by overworking the physical.

The 'Yes, But...Theory' simplifies applying mental training to young athletes.

Another reason mental training has been withheld from today's teams, is coaches see the mental and physical as being separate training programs.

Coaches can purchase books on baseball hitting, basketball shooting, golf swing, etc. In other books they find programs for training their athletes mentally. As a result, it's considered to be two different programs, requiring different training sessions.

This is a misconception. Consider this.

The goal of a physical training program is the same as that of mental training—to shorten the distance between what a player is presently doing and what he's capable of doing.

The success of each depends on the same outcome—player improvement.

Physical training is considered to be one of teaching fundamentals and organization, while the mental preparation is to direct the thought process. This appears to be two different programs, but for either training to be successful, a basketball player must shoot and dribble better, a baseball player must hit and throw better, and a golfer must hit farther and straighter. Success for either depends on the same thing.

For a baseball player to hit a fast ball, he must be prepared both mentally and physically. He must be able to swing the bat, but before his muscles will work smoothly and coordinated, he must believe he is capable.

A coach wanting to teach him to hit the ball better will want him swinging a bat at a ball. Why? Because that's the fundamental he's wanting to improve. Then, to train his mental game, why take him to some deserted room with neither a bat nor a ball. The aim is to help him with his hitting.

Wouldn't it be better to train him while he's performing the fundamental he's wanting to perfect?

A good training program is a single program where the physical and mental are taught simultaneously.

Mental and physical training are like boyfriend and girlfriend; most of the time they walk hand-in-hand.

15. How To Use The 'Theory'

A successful season begins with thoughts of success.

There's a ghost in your midst.

It's surrounding your youngsters, your team and you.

No one has ever seen it. But we have all seen the havoc the invisible "ghost" has created.

It attacks with various methods, and challenges with persistency.

The ghost is the 'Destroyer of Success'; it's the 'Killer of Consistency'.

Among its weapons are doubt, fear, confusion, anxiety and apprehension.

No one is immune from its attacks. All must daily stand 'toe-to-toe' and battle this challenger to succeed. If we tuck tail and run, success will only be a dream.

This ghost hates success, and will do every thing within its means to cause players to be so tense and so filled with lack of confidence that peak performance is impossible.

Some youngsters have developed strong armor to ward off the blows this Destroyer of Success hurls. But many stand defenseless before it, hammered down with each attack, until they run for protective cover, giving up hopes of success.

Why one possesses a strong suit of protection, while others must stand naked before this challenger, may be unknown to everyone, but one thing is known—it's possible to create an armor for those who don't have one.

> **NOTE**
> Some players are super confident and nothing seems to shake them, while others are bothered by almost every little thing. Why these personalities have been developed may be unknown, but we do know players' degree of confidence can be altered. This is one aim of the 'Theory'—to improve confidence.

This ghost doesn't aim its weapons toward the physical ability to play the game, but focuses on the emotions, which is the surest and quickest method of disrupting effective performance.

Although these threats are directed toward the emotions, the effects are seen in the players' performance. Since it is evident the physical is being performed below expectations, all effort to correct the problem is often directed at the player's ability rather than the emotions.

It's almost impossible to correct the mental game by stressing physical improvement.

It would be diffucult to change fear into courage by spending an extra hour working on fundamental drills.

You must understand efficient play depends on a 'partnership'. The partners are the physical (body) and mental (emotional).

Trying to remedy a confidence problem by working on the physical, would be like having a team of horses with only one horse pulling. You just can't make Old Nellie pull by whipping Old Ned. Old Nellie must be the one receiving the encouragement.

DON'T FEAR THE MIND'S COMPLEXITY

Many times we abuse the wrong partner because we feel inadequate to deal with anything associated with the workings of the mind.

Since emotions, such as fear, doubt and confidence, are classified as being 'of the mind', we shy away from dealing with them.

Granted, the mind is a super complex creation. It's so complex the most learned scientist has probably only scratched the surface in understanding its capabilities.

But, developing a positive attitude in athletics doesn't require an in-depth knowledge of the mind's operation. You don't have to be a psychologist or psychiatrist, and you don't have to worry about 'messing up' someone's mind.

You and your youngsters are going to have self-thoughts. These thoughts will either be 'good thoughts' or 'bad thoughts'.

The only objective of the "Yes, But...Theory' is to emphasize the good feelings while degrading the bad, and what could be "psychologically unhealthy" about that? What could be wrong with trying to get yourself or your youngsters to think good rather than bad?

This trait isn't far from being a necessity of life.

Success hinges on thinking of the good. This is the basis of self-confidence, and no one would disagree that confidence is necessary for championship performance.

Confidence can be compared to a large water bottle. When the bottle is full, confidence is at its maximum. When it's empty, confidence is gone.

Every good thought or feeling we have about ourselves puts a drop into the bottle, and each bad feeling siphons it out.

For confidence to grow, there must be more good feelings than bad.

PSYCHOLOGICAL PRINCIPLES

To direct your youngster into a positive way of life, there are only a few psychological principles you need to know.

It has already been mentioned that MORE GOOD THAN BAD THOUGHTS LEAD TO A CONFIDENT LIFE, WHILE THE OPPOSITE CAUSES A NEGATIVE ATTITUDE.

The second principle is, THE MIND CAN ONLY THINK ONE THING AT A TIME. It can switch back and forth from one thought to another, but only one will be there at a time.

The third is, THE MIND WILL CONCENTRATE ON WHATEVER IS CONSIDERED TO BE THE MOST IMPORTANT. This doesn't mean it will be there 100 percent of the time. Our thoughts will switch to other things not so important, but the most important will occupy our thoughts the majority of the time. And, that's what we're concerned about—the majority of the thoughts.

If we think more good thoughts than bad thoughts, the 'confidence' bottle will be filled. If bad feelings are our major thoughts, confidence will eventually be drained off.

Therefore, if these three principles are correct, then: If we can make good feelings about ourselves the most important, we will think of them the most, and our self-evaluation and confidence will grow.

(From now on this will be referred as THE PREMISE.)

THINK GOOD TO BE GOOD

This premise goes along with a suggestion the Apostle Paul gave, in the Bible, to the people of Philippi. He said; "Whatsoever things are true, whatsoever things are honest, whatsoever things are just, whatsoever things are pure, whatsoever things are lovely, whatsoever things are of good report; if there be any virtue, and if there be any praise, think on these things." (Philippians 4:8)

Imagine how good and clean a person would be if these were the only kinds of thoughts he ever had.

Imagine how confident a young person would be if he only had good thoughts about his ability!

It would be ridiculous to assume we could ever lead our youngsters to a point where no negatives would ever enter their minds. That would be impossible, but it's even more ridiculous to leave them to the mercy of self-defeating thoughts without trying to give them help.

They deserve more than you having a 'hands off' attitude toward their way of thinking. You're obligated to offer them every bit of expertise you have to train them to see the good they have within themselves. They can be trained to believe in themselves, and it is your responsibility to lead them as close to perfect confidence as possible.

Everyone knows that thinking good thoughts will increase confidence, but the 'hang-up' comes when they began trying to apply a mental training program to their situation.

Application of the premise isn't difficult, nor time consuming.

The idea behind the premise has been used for years with good success. It was never given a name. It was just a coaching philosophy, but to help

How To Use The 'Theory' 119

WE PLAYED WELL, BUT LOST.

IF	IF
concentration is on losing, then	concentration is on playing well, then

| Downcast attitude, and next performance may suffer. | Pleased, with a positive outlook for the next contest. |

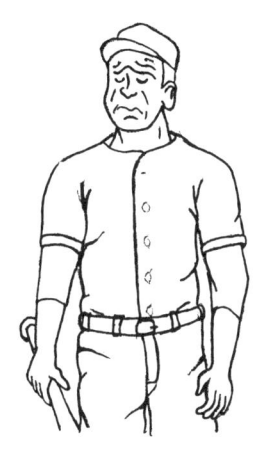

understand it, it will be called the 'Yes, But...Theory'.

Applying the premise to your young person or team will be explained a step at a time.

STEP ONE 'YES'

When anyone, child or adult, confronts a problem, there is a certain degree of apprehension and anxiety.

Since these emotional conditions restrict good, smooth, muscular motion, peak performance can't be expected. Nervousness and worry must be eliminated before maximum potential can be reached.

It's imperative anxieties be erased as quickly as possible. The longer they're allowed to remain, the more damage they'll do, and the harder it will be to get back to normal. Trying to bury them in the mind, or attempting to deny they exist, isn't the correct approach.

A problem must be attacked. It must be challenged with as much vengence and viciousness as we would an enemy who is out to destroy us, because if left unchecked, that's what problems will eventually do—they will destroy our athletic career.

If we hide it, or deny its existence, we won't develop a plan of attack. We can't attack what, to us, isn't there.

The best way to begin ridding ourselves of a problem is to admit it's there. Say, "Yes, I have a problem." Get it out in the open; out front, where a plan of attack can be formulated.

Also, it creates less anxiety to admit it is there than it does to deny it.

STEP TWO 'DEGRADE THE PROBLEM'

Survival! Nothing is more important to us.

Mankind, and all living species, were created with a natural desire for self-preservation. Without it, all living things would become extinct.

Nothing arouses us more than having our existence threatened.

This desire for continued existence isn't limited to just our lives. It spills over into anything that's a part of us—our families, homes, happiness and careers.

When athletic careers are threatened, the natural desire to survive 'kicks in'.

How To Use The 'Theory'

Threats to survival bring fear.

Fear is important to the continued existence of any living things. If birds weren't naturally afraid of cats, we would soon have a lot of fat cats, but few birds singing. If the cave men hadn't been afraid of the wild animals, the human race would have disappeared before we were born, and, today, if we weren't afraid of guns and speeding 18-wheelers bearing down on us, we would have no great-grandchildren.

But, we've carried this natural emotional trait too far.

Losing a ball game is not a threat to survival; missing a freethrow at a crucial time in a game doesn't bring extinction; and a dropped football or missed tackle doesn't carry the death penalty.

Athletics at the professional level is the player's livelihood, and should be approached more seriously. But, for the young person, playing must be kept in the correct perspective—it needs to be enjoyed.

> **NOTE**
>
> 1. When an athletic performance is threatened, fear develops.
>
> 2. Fear automatically makes the situation important to a young person.
>
> 3. Since the mind dwells on the most important,
>
> 4. the threat is the main thought running through the mind.

A young boy or girl can't be expected to give a good performance with fear and threatening thoughts raging through their mind. It's impossible.

Criticism and threats of punishment won't solve the problem, but will probably increase it. Understanding and leadership is needed. THEY NEED THE IMPORTANCE OF THE SITUATION DEGRADED. They need the threat reduced to the point it no longer dominates the thinking.

Only then will the emotions allow the body to relax enough to play up to its potential.

Step one in attacking a problem is to admit it. Say, "Yes, I have a problem." This eliminates any conflict of trying to hide it or deny its existence, and opens the door for a plan that will destroy its importance.

Step two is to degrade it— decrease its power to harm.

A good way to start this process is to follow the admitting of a problem with the word 'BUT'.

If a player hadn't been playing very well for the last three or four games, and said, "Yes, I haven't been playing well," he wouldn't be trying to hide or deny it, but it would still be a strong, frightening statement.

But, if the player said, "Yes, I haven't been playing well lately, BUT...", the statement isn't so demeaning. The word 'but' qualifies a preceding statement. In this case it makes it sound like he is saying, "I haven't been playing well, but there is really no need to get excited, because..."

PROVE THE NEGATIVE IS UNIMPORTANT

If the player could find a statement which would give proof there's no need to get overly excited, the importance of the problem (not playing well) would be degraded.

Finding a 'proving' statement isn't as difficult as it may seem. Every person, situation and event has both good and bad sides.

Players with super confidence have developed a way of seeing the good, and then concentrating on it. Those who are timid and doubtful, always seem to see the bad.

Both those who see the good and those who see the bad, have been trained to do so. It's almost impossible to point out when or why either developed the habit of thinking the way they do, but experiences and situations through their lives have caused them to be as they are. Even most parents can only guess the reason their child reacts a certain way.

Again, everyone can be 'retrained'.

To retrain them, we must get them in a habit of finding a positive statement to follow the word 'because' to prove the problem isn't too serious.

The 'Yes, But...Theory' could be called the 'Yes, But...Because Theory'. Yes is admitting the problem exists; but is feeling it isn't extra important; and because is giving proof it isn't too important.

In most situations, the proof is there and can be found, if the player will

How To Use The 'Theory' 123

only search for it.

Some examples of proof are:

✔ Being in a slump isn't too bad, because they are usually only temporary and will pass.

(Thoughts of the slump not being permanent, and normal play returning is more important than the 'temporary slump'.)

✔ Failing to make the starting team isn't too bad when you consider you are still part of the team, can contribute to the success and have the privilege of improving and moving up.

(Being a contributing part of something you love is more important than not being 'top dog'.)

✔ Making a mistake isn't too bad, because everyone makes them. They are a part of athletics.

✔ Losing a match or game isn't bad considering we learn more from errors and losses than we do wins. Losses give us an opportunity to learn.

(Losses and failures are our 'roadmap' to improvement, and improvement is our ride to success. Some coaches consider them to be necessities to reaching your best. Also, nothing is more self-satisfying in any contest than knowing you gave your best.)

✔ The importance of winning and losing isn't so great, considering the most memorable parts of youth sports is the relationships with coaches, players, and fans. Winning isn't necessary to have these memories.

(In later years, your recollection of your association with the team and opponents will be far more important than your wins and losses.)

✔ Striking out in the bottom of the last inning with the winning runs on base is not nearly as important as knowing you gave your team the best you had to offer.

✔ Failing to come through victoriously in a close game is not such a big deal when you consider the uncertainty of the outcome of any contest is what makes the game interesting.

(If the outcome of any sport was predetermined, interest would fade and the sport would die. No one who prepares diligently for a contest, and plays his best during the game is a loser. There is no greater victory than having pride in the way you prepared and played.)

✔ Being too short isn't nearly as important when you understand teams need much more than height to be successful.

✔ Being too slow is not as important as being dedicated, determined and having a lot of hustle.

The list could go on and on, but each situation has its own personality, and that will dictate where to look for the thought to neutralize the negative.

NEUTRALIZING STATEMENTS

Some examples of neutralizing (or degrading) statements are:

✔ Yes, I fumbled the ball, but it isn't too important, because normally I don't do that, and I learned from it, and it will make me a better player.

(Not my normal self is the most important thought)

✔ Yes, I made a bad pitch, which was hit for a home run, but I won't worry about it, because I know I'm a good pitcher. I did my best and everyone makes mistakes. The batter was better than me this time, but next time I will be more careful.

(I'm a good pitcher is more important than I made a bad pitch.)

✔ Yes, I missed a shot right under the goal, but the most important thing is that I'm better than that. I may not miss another one like that the rest of the season.

(I'll probably make all of the others is more important than I missed one in the past.)

Two of the most effective neutralizing statements are the ones based on 'I'm better than that' or 'I'm improving'.

Always remember that the mind can only think one thing at a time, and it will be a thought that is the most important to us.

When facing a problem, the key is to give our minds two thoughts from which to choose—the problem and a positive. Alway make sure the positive is more important than the negative.

The more this is done, the easier it will be to bring a positive to mind. It's like working on fundamentals, the more it's practiced, the more perfect it will become.

16.
Satellite View Of The 'Theory'

Improvement comes from shortening the distance between what we're doing and what we're capable of doing.

In Part One, "Plan To Win", we looked at the mental training theory close-up, viewing its use in individual situations. Now we will back off and examine its overall philosophy.

Don't think of the 'Theory' as some gimmick to be used in special situations when youngsters face tough times.

It's more than that. It's an attitude; a frame of mind. It governs the way coaches, parents and players react to everyday, serious and incidental situations.

It's a way of thinking that can help anyone stop emphasizing those everyday negatives that rain on us all.

Rather than visualizing a player attacking individual problems, see him with a personality that automatically causes him to react positively.

Don't imagine a coach running around saying, "Yes, but..." all the time, but envision him with the attitude that problems should be admitted, and then degraded with good thoughts. See him passing this on to his players through his coaching methods.

See players and coaches who know they have problems, but feel they have more good than bad happening to them.

The big picture isn't players and coaches challenging individual problems, but people who react to threats automatically. It's just their way of life.

These attitudes don't happen overnight. They develop over a period of time.

Although results can be seen almost immediately in some situations, this isn't a quick-fix program, but one that opens the door to growth.

It aids the personality of coaches' and players' to grow until it habitually focuses on the good while discarding the bad.

In the first weeks of using the program, the personality will continually need to search for a positive to neutralize a negative feeling, but will grow until it automatically brings positive thoughts to mind.

The way we think is a habit developed over time. This program encourages us to make thinking of the good our habit.

Since it has been proven beyond any reasonable doubt that we are what we think we are, it's important our self-thought be the best possible.

WHAT COACHING STYLE DOES THE 'THEORY' REQUIRE?

The style a coach chooses to use is immaterial to the 'Theory'. It will fit perfectly with any.

An athlete following this program will be concentrating on how he is playing, not how the game is played.

If your offensive preference is a high tempo, wide open one, this program will work as well as it would with a deliberate one.

It doesn't matter if your program is based on extreme discipline or player freedom, the program will adapt to either.

Coaching style doesn't have to be altered.

This is not a 'style' of coaching, but an 'attitude' toward performance.

Your coaching style, whether wide open or deliberate, and your discipline, whether strict or loose, doesn't change the fact that the more confident a player is, the more apt he is to be successful.

This 'Theory' is to change the way a player thinks about himself, rather than how he feels about a style of play.

METHOD OF PRESENTING THE 'THEORY'

Three ways to use this program include:
1. Inform and educate the players on the program.

The players have the program outlined to them just as it has been in this book. They're encouraged to participate in formulating all counteracting statements.

2. Don't tell the players and lead them by coaching.

When this method is chosen, none of the players are taught, 'important thought', 'counteracting negatives', 'admitting problems', etc. Parents and coaches "show" the players how to feel about their performance, by the attitude they have, and how they react to situations.

Parents and coaches should always use this method regardless of the method they choose for the youngsters.

3. Privately inform part of the players and lead the others by example.

The players whom the coach feels are having trouble with self-confidence, will have the program explained in counseling sessions. The others will be led by parent or coach examples.

Regardless of the method chosen, the coach and parent must understand that they can choose which method to use for their young boys and girls, but they have no choice for their own actions. It's imperative leaders take an active role in helping youngsters develop belief in themselves. Some type mental training must be offered.

AUTHOR'S NOTE

I've used all three methods of presentation, but I prefer and recommend the first, informing all players.

I suggest this because it gives the players an opportunity to improve their confidence 24-hours a day. When leading by example, the opportunities you have to train them are limited. Also, we don't always know another's thoughts. After the program has been explained and they've gained some experience using it, they can, with help, develop a more effective plan against negatives.

Just make sure you don't explain it to them and then forget your responsibility. No matter how proficient they get at using it, they still need your encouragement and support. Continue as their leader in both the mental training program, and in fundamental improvement.

You can't be a non-influential part of your child or team. You're either a positive or negative influence, whether you like it or not. Make it positive.

IS THIS PAMPERING YOUNGSTERS?

It isn't the intention of this program to 'baby' players in any way.

Coaches shouldn't be required to wipe noses and powder behinds, but failure to lead can't be justified by any ethical standards.

Mental training is leading. It is leading, not only to athletic success, but also to happiness, contentment and better emotional stability.

Coaches and parents can be demanding and still lead youngsters to confidence without 'petting' them.

Responsibility and acting their age should be demanded of players, but they should be led in that direction.

Any mental training program provides an opportunity to coach a player 'up' rather than 'down'.

Being demanding shouldn't harm a player's self-image, but many times degrading, demeaning and threatening statements by a coach or a parent can undo in a few minutes what took months to build.

This is coaching a player down.

Demanding responsibility and good conduct while leading toward self-confidence is coaching up.

IMPROVEMENT—THE KEY TO SUCCESS

When the season begins, the most influential factor determining whether a team will make the play-offs is often improvement.

Without improvement, a team is chained to its present level of play. The only way they can move up the ladder of success is for the opposition to become less capable, and with the spirit of competition today, that's unlikely.

Failing to improve may not only keep your team from moving up, but improvement by other teams may actually cause you to fall in the standing.

MAKE IMPROVEMENT A GOAL

Setting goals is not included in this book, but there is one goal every individual and team should strive to reach—daily improvement.

It should be everyone's goal to come out of every practice better than they were when practice began.

It's universally accepted that performance is never constant. It's always changing. If it isn't getting better, it will get worse. It will never remain the same.

This gives strength to the saying, 'Improvement doesn't have to be great, but it does need to be steady'. Improvement, no matter how small, is better than going backward.

Improvement can be compared to a roller coaster that leaves the loading area on Monday. It goes up during periods of hope and encouragement and down when doubt and fear are present. Friday, when it comes back to the loading area, it's at exactly the same level it was at the beginning of the week.

In this example, improvement wasn't constant. It was continually changing. The problem was, improvement gains and losses were equal, so performance potential ended up right where it started on Monday.

A week without any advancement does nothing for play-off hopes.

The roller coaster analogy is the story of most struggling teams. All a good practice session accomplishes is recover previous losses; getting back to a level they've already held.

Practice time is limited. Every day we spend climbing back after sliding down, is a day wasted.

These ups and downs in performing fundamentals are usually caused by mental factors.

The 'Theory' can help stop those down-turns in capabilities by:

1. Counteracting negatives with positives.

2. Stopping players from concentrating on their weaknesses and failures.

3. Helping develop a good attitude toward the sport and self.

Barring injury or sickness, a person's physical ability to carry out fundamental activities will fluctuate very little from week to week. Varying of potential depends on whether the mind is working with the body or interfering with it.

We all have both negative and positive thoughts. The one we make the most important and listen to will have the greatest influence on us.

The position the mind takes results from the thoughts we hold. Good, encouraging thoughts lead to the mind working with the body. Fear, doubt and turmoil causes interference.

It's time we train young athletes to intercept and neutralize their negative thoughts and problems; replace doubts with positive beliefs; fear with hope.

Start by explaining this 'Theory'. Next, have them consciously admit their problems and find a positive to counteract it. Lead and encourage them until doing this becomes a habit and a way of life.

You may not be able to lead them to be completely free of frustration and self-doubt, but every little bit you accomplish has the possibility of making a major difference in their lives.

INNER CONFLICT

Conflict is a coach's nightmare; parents' wrath; fans' anger; and a sure sign of less-than-best performance.

It has been the ruination of teams ranging from a Saturday afternoon 'pick-up' game of basketball to professional baseball teams hoping for a World Series title.

Conflict can be between two players, or between coach and players. It can be given birth by parents, fans, administration or the local press, but no matter who originated it, it's always damaging to a team's hopes.

When conflicts occur, everyone focuses their attention on them, and will do all that's possible to smooth them out. Even team members who aren't involved join in because they know it's jeopardizing their success, too.

There is another conflict. It has dashed more team hopes on the rocks than all the others combined, yet little effort is made to correct it.

This is the conflict players have within themselves.

Many players wage a continual argument in their minds.

It's like a cartoon with an angel on one shoulder, encouraging good deeds, and a little devil on the other, suggesting mischief.

Real life isn't much different. One argument in the player's mind says he can; another says he can't, and he's caught in the middle 'wondering' which is right.

Wondering is a form of doubt, and championship performance and doubt don't go hand-in-hand.

Going into a game wondering, is having the mental picture out of focus. In trying to focus, they only catch glimpses of it. The first glimpse they get, they think their mental picture was painted brightly. The next glimpse looks dull and smudged. The picture is usually evaluated dimmer than it really is, so performance suffers.

If a championship is lost because Jim and Bob are having a spat and won't work together, everyone is in an uproar. It seems senseless to them that the other team got the trophy because two of their own players were fighting.

But, if a championship is lost because Bill 'wasn't hitting' and didn't have his normal game, or if Mary was nervous and played below her average, we pass this off as 'just being the way sports are'.

Both games were actually lost for the same reason—conflict. One was conflict between two different players; the other, conflict within one player.

Both were largely responsible for losing the game and both are correctable.

Conflict comes from placing emphasis on negatives.

Jim, Bob, or both emphasized some negative in their relationship to create the fight between them. Bill and Mary did the same with something in their own lives.

If Jim and Bob had settled their differences, they may have been the champions.

If Bill and Mary had been trained to make the good the most important in their thoughts, the trophy may have been setting in their school's display case instead of their opponent's.

A few championships are lost because of conflict between players or coaches, and all-out effort is directed at preventing it.

Nearly all championship games are influenced by conflict within the players' own minds, and hardly anything is done about that.

It doesn't make sense, does it, to go all-out to prevent what happens occasionally, and ignore what happens in almost every contest?

A good mental training program will help players find and concentrate on good, strong positive thoughts, and there is no better way of calming players' internal conflict.

PUTTING THE 'THEORY' IN GEAR

Don't develop an image of this program as something sophisticated that would take half your instruction time.

It's simple and will require almost no extra time, additional equipment or personnel.

Throughout the book (especially in the story part) all hypothetical problems were challenged using the 'Yes, But...Theory'. This was to make sure the foundation of this training was understood.

> **FOUNDATION REVIEW**
>
> Don't deny problems exist; admit them. Since what we think about influences playing, the problem musn't be our main thought. This is accomplished by offering our thoughts two choices— the problem, and a positive that's more important to us.

Our mind can only think of one thing at a time and will choose the most important as its major thought.

Positive thoughts lead to positive play.

Yes, But..., is the foundation of the program, but it's not necessary to state the neutralizers everytime.

There is nothing wrong with either mentally, or out loud, going through the entire neutralizing statement. In fact, in the early weeks of using the 'Theory', this is recommended, but later players will find it isn't necessary.

After gaining experience using it, they will automatically draw a positive thought to their minds from ones used in the past. Every positive thought they formulate will be mentally filed away. These can be brought to the surface of their thoughts almost effortlessly.

The more counteracting statements formed, the larger the file, and the easier it will be to remember an appropriate one.

If players work at this hard enough, it's possible they'll eventually reach a point where they'll react this way to negatives without thought or effort. It will be their natural way of approaching situations.

However, players should be warned this can be attained only by applying dedicated and determined effort. Two things must be accomplished. First, a habit of thinking negatively must be broken. Second, a habit of thinking positively must be developed.

Most authorities on human behavior would agree it takes at least two or three weeks to break a habit or develop a new one, even with dedicated effort.

It isn't easy to reject negatives automatically, but what is a few weeks compared to a lifetime of pleasant memories of one's school athletic career?

Coaches and Parents, your youngster, like all of us, is a creature of habit. What we do by habit, we do the easiest, and no matter how dedicated they are to thinking good self-thoughts, they will veer from the path occasionally.

They need you to be alert for signs of their reverting and allowing some negative to dominate their thinking. They need your prodding and encouragement to keep them heading in the correct direction.

No matter how much they want to improve their way of thinking, habit will occasionally rule over desire.

It will take effort on your part, but again, what is a few weeks' effort compared to memories and satisfaction?

17.
A Few Suggestions

**Those who never try, never fail.
They also seldom succeed.**

REACH FOR THE STARS

Success comes to those who see the possibility of disappointment in front of them, but continue anyway.

The chance of meeting disappointment mustn't be avoided, but faced head on, because it's almost impossible to reach success without risking failure.

Always choosing the safe road isn't advisable. That usually means giving up on the opportunity to succeed.

Unfortunately, many discard high hopes fearing failure. They feel that if they never hope for good things, they won't be discouraged when it doesn't happen.

Motivated by a desire to protect their children, parents often discourage them from aiming high. They're afraid the children may suffer a letdown if they fail to reach the goal. It's easy to become an overprotective parent.

Coaches have led teams away from challenges that stand between them and success. Seeing only the possible disappointment, they fail to see the potential for achievement.

If the challenge isn't met, present disappointment will probably be avoided, but so will the chance at success.

It's true, disappointment is more apt to come to those who set high goals than it is to those who set goals they know they can reach, but we can't always avoid the rough road. Challenging goals can lead to frustration, but can also lead to huge triumphs.

Disappointment and success come only to those who try. Those who never try, never fail. They, also, seldom succeed.

AIM HIGH

Aiming low is almost certain to bring limited success. Very seldom does one reach higher than his aim.

A high jumper who sets a goal of six feet may reach it, but most likely not exceed it. A jumper who sets a goal of seven feet and six inches may fail to reach his goal, but may jump seven feet because of the effort he put out.

Ask yourself which is better—aiming at six feet and hitting it, or aiming at seven feet and six inches and hitting seven feet?

Failing to reach a goal doesn't always mean failure. Disappointment and success can both be experienced in the same situation.

The jumper trying for seven-six and reaching seven may be disappointed because he never reached his goal, but jumping seven is clearly a victory.

To be state semi-finalist is a triumph, but disappointing when the goal was to be state champion.

The letdown will only last a short time, but the memory of achievement will last throughout the years.

More importantly, the player who worked hard to reach a high goal and failed, will always know what he was capable of accomplishing. He knows because he gave his all and reached his best.

On the other hand, the jumper who reached six feet will never know what he was capable of doing. For the rest of his life he will have to look back and wonder what he could have done if he had only made the effort.

Side-stepping present possible discouragements may give birth to questions that last a lifetime.

When a season or career has ended, the greatest and most lasting disappointment is having to look back and say, "It might have been."

Step out on the limb. There may be disappointments there, but one thing is for sure, it's the only place true success can be found.

Conservative goals bring conservative gains.

NEVER GIVE UP!

Sir Winston Churchill, a great prime minister of England, in an address at Harrow School, said, "Never give in, never give in, never, never, never, never—in nothing, great or small, large or petty—never give in."

What better advice to anyone.

Until we give up, we have hope.

When we give up, we have no hope.

Without hope, we have nothing.

As long as we have hope, we will continue our efforts to succeed, and as long as we are trying, success is possible.

Once we give up, we will cease all efforts to win.

When our efforts cease, defeat is almost 100 percent certain.

Never give up!!

THE GREAT WASTE

'You only go around once' is a commonly heard statement.

It's message is true.

With only one life to live, what could be a greater waste than living it unhappily?

It would be nice if this only happens occasionally. But it doesn't. It's happening by the millions.

It would be nice if very few young athletes were wasting the few years they have in athletics. It would be nice if most young athletes were getting the maximum enjoyment from their short playing time. But, unfortunately, these scenarios keep happening, too.

It's a waste when the one 'shot' doesn't end up satisfying.

The waste is sad when the loss couldn't have been prevented, but even sadder when it was avoidable.

In life or in athletics, maximum satisfaction or success finds it hard to work its way into anyone's life who habitually emphasizes the bad and ignores the good.

Young people who have the habit of always seeing the down side, stand a big risk of living an unhappy life, but it isn't written in stone that they must live with this habit the rest of their lives. Habits can be broken and new ones developed.

Those who have decided they aren't capable, or are no good, need to be made aware there is good in all situations, and in all people. They need to be trained to find that good, and substitute those thoughts for their bad feelings.

It needs to be explained to them that their minds can only think one thing at a time, and that the one thought will be what is most important to them.

They need to be reminded and stay aware that they've made a habit of making the bad the most important, but that that can be changed. It's possible to redecide what is the most important in life.

They need this explanation, and more. They need leadership. They need your encouragement, and the continual support your everyday remarks and statements can give.

A high school psychology student said it this way, when suggesting a class on 'redeciding' should be required of all students: "Everyone knows where he or she is weak or having trouble, but most don't realize they have the chance to change what isn't right in their lives."

Help them change by helping them find and think on the good in their lives.

WINNING AND LOSING

If the question, "How important is winning?", were presented to 100 people there would probably be 100 different answers. The answers would range from: "Emphasizing winning puts too much pressure on young players" to "Losing is worse than death because you have to live with losing."

In too many cases winning does carry too much weight. When we get to the point winning equals success and losing equals failure, we've gone too far.

When enjoyment only comes from victory, we need to stop and look.

Clean competition is healthy in many ways. It's a healthy attitude to care whether one wins or loses. Without this, interest in the game would quickly fade. Also, we're faced with competition throughout our lives and much of the quality of life we have depends on how we compete.

But, the importance of any athletic program is based on more than wanting to win. Developing good relationships with other teammates,

A Few Suggestions

coaches, fans and opponents must be included in any athlete's aim.

Any player should look with favor on the challenges of athletic competition. Some of these challenges come from within and others from opponents.

No athlete should discount the character-building benefits possible from a good program.

To win within the bounds of good sportsmanship must be a main objective of any athletic program. Everyone needs to be taught to strive for excellence. To do otherwise would be wrong, but it can be carried so far it becomes unhealthy.

Any athlete or athletic team should set high goals. They should work hard and have high expectations of reaching them.

What's important is the attitude held after the season when the goal has or hasn't been reached.

A healthy approach would be to set high goals, work hard to achieve them and be able to accept the outcome whatever it might be. Don't be remorseful when losing and don't overdo the winning celebration.

A player who overemphasizes winning will care too much about losing, and this could cause anxiety.

Anxiety and frustrations are unhealthy.

There is a lot of truth in the statement 'Don't get too high when winning, nor too low when losing'. A player who gets abnormally elated when winning or exceptionally depressed when losing, is setting himself up for an unhealthy career. With this attitude, losing becomes a threat, and with it much of the enjoyment vanishes.

This is not to say the desire to win should be depressed. The will to win encourages a player to work hard and persistently.

When winning becomes so important to the player that the desire to win and fear of losing causes tenseness and nervousness, the goals must be reexamined.

FEELING OF INFERIORITY

Dealing with a player's feeling of inferiority is a complex question to answer. Many times when coaches gather, they puzzle over it, but find it practically impossible to answer because inferiority comes in many degrees.

Everyone is inferior and superior to all others in some respect.

A Few Suggestions

Every person is, in one way or another inferior to others. It's impossible to find anyone who is superior in every respect. Each one of us has someone 'superior' to us in some trait or skill.

In sports, inferiority becomes a problem when the player feels threatened, ashamed or feels he can't measure up to what he and his peers expect.

Players who realize everyone is inferior, usually aren't affected by their own inferior traits. Players who have 'feelings of inferiority' are the ones whose performance suffers.

It's not the knowledge of being inferior that bothers us, but the 'feelings' we have about being inferior.

This goes right along with a statement made throughout the book: How we feel affects how we play.

Young people have a tendency to rate themselves according to another's potential. Invariably there will be some part of the other person's ability that will be better than their own. The result—inferiority feelings.

Tell them, "You are you. There is none other like you."

Explain to your youngsters that when they compare themselves with others they can always find traits indicating they are inferior. They can also find evidence they are superior.

This doesn't mean they're inferior or superior. They are just themselves.

They aren't comparable to anyone else, nor are others comparable to them. Everyone is unique. Everyone has traits that are inferior and superior to every other individual in the world.

Harmless knowledge of being inferior becomes harmful feelings of inferiority when these inferior traits become the most important thought in their mind.

When they compare themselves to others, and find they have some inferior traits, their trouble begins if they concentrate on them.

By doing this, they're emphasizing their weaknesses instead of their strengths.

Everyone has admirable traits. Find them and promote them by making them the most important thoughts.

Your youngster should understand he isn't in competition with others. He is competing with himself.

A CHANGE OF MIND

The single most important factor determining how much a coach or parent helps a youngster improve is: how many positive changes of the mind they can get the young person to make.

Changing the mind from 'I can't, to I can'; 'I doubt I will, to I believe I will'; or 'I'm not important to the team, to I am valuable', will do far more good than any fundamental drill. *Nothing, repeat, nothing is more important to consistent success than the players' self-evaluation.*

Every coach and parent should post this on their bulletin board. They should be required to repeat it aloud 10 times each day before coming in contact with their team or child.

Too often, every possible minute is spent training on the fundamental phase of performance, leaving the self-evaluation to chance.

If their opinion of themselves isn't already positive, leaving it to chance doesn't give them much opportunity to improve.

Leaving to chance what is one of the most important aspects of both their athletic playing days, and their entire lives, is poor leadership.

To help them change their minds, understand them as much as possible. Actively seek to know how they think, what they think, what is important to them, what they believe they can do and what they feel they can't do.

Naturally, you will never have a perfect understanding of them, but by listening to what they say, and watching how they act and react, you will be surprised how close you can come to understanding their feelings about themselves.

These young people have spent their entire lives looking and listening, experiencing success and failure, analyzing other people's actions and beliefs.

All these things have been filed away in their 'mental filing room'.

There is more in these files than could be put into a house full of filing cabinets, but the mind can categorize and go through it in a fraction of a second.

We learn by association, so everything that happens to us is associated with something already in our mind's file.

Suppose a young lady playing basketball makes a particular maneuver and shoots the ball. How she rates this will depend on what she draws from her mental file.

A Few Suggestions

If the move was better than what she has been accustomed to doing, she may rate it as luck, or maybe something she occasionally does. Either way, she won't rate it as being her normal self and won't expect it to happen again.

Expecting it 'not to happen', almost guarantees it won't.

The important thing to remember is that there are other mental files she could have gone to for her association, but being creatures of habit, we usually go back to the same files.

We have files and files that are completely dust covered and hardly ever opened. Others are worn shiny from being opened and closed so often.

If these files of habit indicate success, we're fortunate. If they don't, we're headed for rocky roads.

Some statements parents and coaches could use to train this basketball player to go to other files are: 'Hey, you're getting better', 'Say, those drills you've been running are showing up in your performance, aren't they?', 'You didn't know you were that good, did you?', or 'I knew you were going to start making the move that way'.

Remarks like these indicate success rather than luck. Feelings of success brightens a mental picture, while images of luck keep it dim.

Making statements like these only a few times won't be sufficient to change their minds. Remember, they have a habit of going to the same file cabinet, and it takes weeks to change a habit.

> **NOTE**
>
> Coaches and parents should mark this section of the book. The importance of success-suggesting remarks can't be over-emphasized. It should be noted, however, that the statements must be reasonable (believable). They must be ones which can be associated with something already in their minds. Study this and, based on your youngster's situation, have some remarks ready for the next practice session. Be prepared!!

THE PARTNERSHIP CIRCLE

Any young athlete's success depends largely on a partnership.

The partnership is three-way—The player, the parents and the coach.

To illustrate, picture the three partners standing in a circle. Each member is standing next to the other two. No one is separated from the others.

In a line, someone would have to be at the head and someone at the end. Also, whoever was standing in the middle would be separating the other two.

The goal of all three is the same—to make the athlete the best he or she can be.

The partnership, like all others, needs cooperation before maximum success can be reached, but often it's like many business partnerships, there's arguing, disagreements and criticisms. As a result, no one reaches his goal.

There are many ways the partnership can become divided. The parent and player divided against the coach; parent standing between the player and the coach; or maybe the player feels all decisions are made by the parent and coach, and he or she has no say in the partnership.

Coaches should realize that parents love their son or daughter and wants the best possible for them. And, yes, sometimes the parent will be biased, but one thing is certain, working with parents will be more productive than working against them.

The parents must understand the coach has more responsibilities than to their child. He or she must attend to all other players, answer to the school administration, board of education, and has responsibilities to the fans, student body and community. Coaches make mistakes just like everyone else, but most of the time they want what's best for the players.

Most coaches welcome visits from parents if handled appropriately. Meetings can be productive, but when the coach or parent makes threatening statements or criticizes, the partnership will be strained.

All meetings between coaches and parents should be just that—between coach and parent. Neither the coach nor parent should spread news of the meeting throughout the community.

Both parent and coach should understand young people have more interests in life than sports. Many times, the player only gets limited consideration, and is treated as an instrument for which the coach and parent gain their enjoyment.

For the partnership to operate smoothly and efficiently the player must be given his or her rightful place in the decisions.

Players should never forget they are members of the partnership and not in this by themselves. Supported by the other two members, they have a responsibility to them. When they fail to do their best, they're letting others down.

Like in any organization, there must be consideration for other members of the partnership, and occasionally, a little give and take is required of all.

18.
One Last Encouragement

Improvement doesn't have to be great... just steady.

As I begin this last chapter, I wish it were possible for me to offer you my hand to personally compliment your sincerity.

I'm confident readers reaching this point are sincere, because all others will have put the book down before getting this far.

The only intention of this book is that it will benefit the reader, whether coach, parent or player. I understand your situation. I've been where you are now. I know what it is to strive for success in the highly-competitive situation all coaches and players find themselves in today.

I love many things about coaching, but the greatest satisfaction I've ever had was seeing players participating with confidence, and enjoying playing, not for the winning or the losing, but for the love of the game and everything that goes with it.

If I had a Genie grant me one wish for the success of this book, I would wish it would lead you to a place of complete enjoyment in your athletic career.

As you near the end of this book, possibly there is a little question running around in your thoughts that's asking, "Is that all there is to it?"

If there is, you're realizing there weren't a lot of ideas presented, but only one idea with several examples and suggestions.

With this one question and realization of the one idea, you should begin understanding that mental training isn't as complicated as many people have thought.

This should point out that it doesn't take a trained sports psychologist to understand the principle that a player who feels good about himself will perform better than one who doesn't.

A person trained in sports psychology could take a player further than this elementary approach to mental training, but this can be of great value as a starting point in any young player or coach in any sport.

Professional training isn't necessary to know that anyone must have good thoughts about self to develop a good attitude. Even an elementary student can visualize how the mind will concentrate on what is the most important to us.

So, the one idea in this book is, when a negative enters our lives, give the mind two thoughts from which to choose, the negative and a more important positive. The mind will emphasize the positive and degrade the negative. Reducing the negative's importance reduces its threat, and this reduces its influence on performance.

Understanding the principle, applying it and finding time to do it, isn't the problem. The lack of extended attention will cause the most failures.

Some folks will begin with good intentions, but will let their minds and interest shift to other things, and their efforts will 'die on the vine' before a habitual pattern of behavior is developed.

With something as important as developing a positive attitude toward life, there is no place to give up; no place to quit.

In fact, it's impossible to quit mental training. We are forever changing our mental picture. If we aren't brightening it, we will be dimming and smudging it. The painting goes on.

Deciding whether to make a habit of painting our picture brighter, or leaving the strokes on the mental canvas to chance, involves more than winning or losing an athletic event. It's winning or losing at life.

Our mental picture goes with us long after athletic competition has passed, and is as influential in the quality of life we lead as in the quality of athletic performance.

What better thing in life could a coach or parent do, than to pour a good foundation for a young person's life. This should be far more satisfying than winning an athletic event.

Developing traits that allow a player to participate under pressure without continual influence of negatives, paves the road to a more poised and confident life.

Remember, we each have only one athletic career and one life. We don't

One Last Encouragement 149

go around twice. Shouldn't we make that 'one shot' as satisfying and successful as possible? With effort, we can PLAN TO WIN!

> For information on consultations, workshops, seminars, etc., contact Glenn Moore, P.O. Box 183, Milburn, Ok 73450, or call 1-405-443-5683.

BIBLIOGRAPHY

Caner, G.C. *It's How You Take It.* New York: Coward-McCann, Inc., 1946.

Dorfman, H.A. & Kuehl, K. *The Mental Game of Baseball: A Guide to Peak Performance.* South Bend, Indiana: Diamond Communications, Inc., 1989.

Durbin, B. *Portrait of a Basketball Player.* Columbus, Kansas: Portrait Publications, 1979.

Fixx, J.F. *Maximum Sports Performance: How to Achieve Your Full Potential in Speed, Endurance, Strength and Coordination.* New York: Random House, 1985.

Gallwey, W.T. *The Inner Game of Tennis.* New York: Random House, 1974.

Garfield, C. A. *Peak Performance: Mental Training Techniques of the World's Greatest Athletes.* New York: Warner Books Inc., 1984.

Harris, D.V. & Harris, B. L. *The Athlete's Guide to Sports Psychology: Mental Skills for Physical People.* New York: Leisure Press, 1984.

Helmstetter, S. *What to Say When You Talk to Yourself.* Scottsdale, Arizona: Grindle Press, 1986.

Hessel, D. *Spirit of Champions: How and Why Athletes Succeed.* Ames, Iowa: Championship Books, 1982.

Loehr, J.E. *Mental Toughness Training for Sports: Achieving Athletic Excellence.* New York: Stephen Greene Press, 1982.

Maltz, M. *Psychocybernetics.* New York: Simon and Schuster, 1960.

Porter, K. & Foster, J. *The Mental Athlete.* New York: Ballantine Books, 1986.

Tutko, T. & Tosi, U. *Sports Psyching: Playing Your Best Game All of the Time.* Los Angeles: T.P. Tarcher, Inc., 1976.

Waitley, D. *The Psychology of Winning: Ten Qualities of a Total Winner*, New York: Berkley Books, 1984.

INDEX

A
Adult Responsibilities, 118, 127-128, 131, 134, 138
Advice
  accepting, 5
  sharing, 5

B
Biblical Beliefs, 62, 118
Blaming Self, 99
But (Importance of), 40, 85-88, 122

C
Choices, 41, 64, 67, 72, 89, 90
Churchill, Winston, 137
Circle of Failure, 37
Coaching Styles, 126
Coaching Success, 4
Coach/Parent Conferences, 144
Compliments, 85, 87
Concentration
  on most important thought, 38
Confidence, 7, 32, 100, 116, 117, 118
Conflict (inner), 35, 37, 63, 122, 131
Counteraction, 53

D
Disappointments, 135-136

Dissension, 97
Doubts and Fears, 17, 90

F
Failing Attitudes, 52
Failure, 45, 135
Fears, 17, 33, 39, 48, 121
  admitting, 35
  attacking, 37
  caused by doubt, 82
  decreasing, 48
  denying, 35
  getting rid of, 34
  justified, 34
  removing, 34, 35, 48
  without threats, 35
Filing System (mind's), 78, 142
Forgetting
  problems, 46
  consciously, 45
  that which is important, 46
Forgiving Self, 62
Friendships, 52
Frustration, 19
Fundamentals, 7, 81, 92
  improvement, 21

G
Goals, 99, 113, 129, 136, 139
Grudges, 63
Guilt Feelings, 60

H
Habits, 19, 81-83, 122, 126, 134
  breaking and creating, 134
  creatures of, 82, 134
Hitch Hiker Athlete, 95
Humility, 5-6

I
Imagery, 25
Improvement, 42, 59, 89, 92 110, 113, 125, 128-129, 147
Inferior Feelings, 139-141
Inner Alarm System, 83

L
Laziness, 97-98
Losing, 51
  attitude toward, 98

M
Meeting Challenges, 135
Mental Game, 109
  defined, 7, 12
Mental Picture, 15, 67, 142
  (also see self-image)
  beginning of, 17
  brightening, 17
  changing, 67-70, 98
  controlling, 18, 21
  ending of, 17
  influence after athletics, 148
  smudging, 17
Mental Training, 53
  being ignored, 112
  failure to offer, 12
  future of, 12
  information on, 112
  unintentional training, 8
  unorganized, 8, 9
Mental Traits, 110-111
Mind/body, 7, 10, 26
Mind's Capabilities, 76
Mind changes, 142
Mind's complexity, 116
Mind's interference, 10, 11

N
Negatives
  challenging, 37
  compared to Trojan Horse, 59
  counteracting, 53, 81
  degrading, 85, 121
  intercepting, 77, 78
  neutralizing, 48
Neutralizing statements, 124
Never giving in, 137

O
Opponent (toughest), 92
Over-reacting, 49

P
Pampering youngsters, 128

Index

Partnership Circle, 144
Performance, 109
  influence of mind, 9, 32
Physical and mental combined, 13
Physical conditioning, 34
Physical traits, 109
Player's rights
  and responsibilities, 145
Poise, 7
Positive attitudes, 55, 82
Positive thinking, 24, 42
  can be negative, 25
Positives (upgrading), 85
Potential vs reality, 97
Potential (waste of), 103, 137
Practice, 57-65, 92
Pride, 5
Problems
  admitting, 63
  attacking, 120
  challenging, 58
  counteracting large, 51, 52
  denying, 41, 120
  everyday, 57
  forgetting, 45-49
  ridding, 120
  running from, 23
  small, 53, 58
  uncontrollable ones, 54

R

Re-deciding, 98, 111, 112, 138

S

Self-evaluation, 111

Self feelings, 16, 67-74
Self-image
  (also see mental picture)
  creating by beliefs, 16, 17, 22, 32, 69
  making it negative, 21
Self-opinion, 16, 17
  creating self-image, 17
Self-talk, 25, 76
  with ideas, 77
  flashing ideas to self, 77
Smiles
  importance of, 101, 102
Standard response, 77, 133
Statements of proof, 122-124
Student (be a) of sport, 89
Success
  in life, 12-13
  striving for, 135
  price of, 95-96
  road to, 91
Success attitudes, 52, 57, 99, 117
Success-suggesting remarks, 143
Survival, 120
  desire for, 39

T

Talent
  use of, 3, 109
Talented players failing, 10
Teacher (be one) of sport, 89
Threats, 121
Three me's, 97
Thoughts, 115
  conflicting, 48
  influence of, 100
  mind holding only one, 38, 117

most important, 47, 48, 119
rejecting, 90
Turmoil, 33

W

Winners (consistent), 6, 7, 8, 89, 109
Winning advantage, 7
Winning and losing, 138-139

Y

Yes, But...Theory
  condensing, 78, 81
  failing, 150
  foundation of, 133
  methods of presentation, 127
  refining, 78, 81

Coach Glenn Moore has coached girls' and boys' basketball and baseball in Oklahoma for twenty-seven years. In girls' basketball alone, he compiled a record of 582 wins with only 179 losses.

In addition to being inducted into the Oklahoma Athletic Hall of Fame, he has been conferred almost every award his Oklahoma coaching association offers.

His teams were always respected for their poise and confidence and his belief that good citizenship and athletic participation go together was recognized when he was selected as Citizen Of The Year by his home county in 1981.